MW01602266

Not All Who Wander are Lost

Not All Who Wander are Lost

A Memoir

An Epic Story about a Man Who went through Hell and Found Himself

Collin Gray

Published by Last Lights Press

Edited by Tim Heerdink

Cover Artwork by Sarah Foley

Author Photo by Emma Paul

Foreword

It goes without saying, addiction can be extremely ugly. However, not every story of an addict ends the way most people might expect it to. Sometimes, in this battle for life, people do overcome addiction and turn their ashes into beauty, giving others hope in such a devastating situation.

Now personally, I always knew Collin would be a world changer. From the moment I met him, I just knew he was a special kind of person. I literally watched this man's life transform right before my very eyes. Broken, battered, and defeated by the trials of life, Collin chose to fight back, giving his life to God and allowing Him to put every broken peace back together again.

Collin reminds me of the mighty Phoenix rising out of the ashes. Our lives are deeply connected because our journeys have been much of the same. This is why I am absolutely honored to write the foreword to his memoir.

As Collin takes you through some of his darkest valleys and onto beautiful mountain tops you will be emotionally taken by his extraordinary journey, as you travel alongside his life, you, too, will become instantly connected with Collin on one level or another.

His words are contagious. Inspired with hope and fueled by love, Collin pulls back the curtains of vulnerability and gives you an intimate look at his life through his faults and failures that are overcome by his strength and determination to truly live.

I hereby place my seal of approval on the work of Collin's hands as every reader is sown into wisdom and truth. I know that you will be blessed as I have been to share such an incredible journey with such a remarkable man. It is true, when God's Holy Spirit is your internal compass, it becomes emphatically clear, that *Not All Who Wander Are Lost*.

Rev. Jeremy C. Touchet

Executive Director and Pastor of Wabash Valley Adult & Teen Challenge

Dedications

This book along with everything else I do is dedicated first and foremost to God my father, Jesus my savior, and the Holy Spirit my guide. Secondly, I want to dedicate this book to my strong, beautiful, and supportive wife and my incredible family. Lastly, I want to dedicate this book to Pastor Jeremy and my counselors from Wabash Valley Teen Challenge. Pastor Keith and his amazing congregation at Cross Tabernacle for pouring out their hearts into my empty cup and being the vehicle in which God used to bring me out of the pits of Hell and into my new Christian life and for that I am going to donate ten percent of the profits I make to WVTC, so they can continue God's work!

Preface

The inspiration I had to write this book came from the Holy Spirit, who no matter how chaotic I've made my life over these years, continues to guide me toward truth and God's light. Also, it's been weighing heavy on my heart that those of you out there whose paths have crossed with this book are living like I once was and that in reading this book you will have the courage to seek God for a better life through His unconditional love.

Firstly, I'm writing this book to show God's glory to the world and then to help those of you living day to day, minute to minute, watching yourselves doing horrible things you never even imagined possible and would give anything to have a redo at life! I wish I had the words to describe my gratitude toward my childhood friends Tim Heerdink with Last Lights Press for helping make this book legible and for helping me publish this book and then Sarah Foley for not only creating this amazing cover art but for also always being a true friend.

Lastly, those of you who I met along my journey and for being there for me and may your souls be at rest. Some of you I met at the gates to Hell, some of you at the deepest depths, and some as I was clawing my way out, but all of you have been life changing in

one way or another. To those I can't personally thank...
I have listed on the next page, have passed on but will
never be forgotten.

Stephen Elkafrawi(Sparta), Samantha (Sky) Riherd, Brian Steiner(Big Poppy), Aaron Brown, William Brewer, Lauren Wallace, Kyle Rickenbaugh, Kelli Peter, Garrett Nelson, Stephen Ford, Josh Boyd(Kazi), Davin Bump, Spencer Meyers, Rachel Smyth, Kelcey Sanders(Ksand), Mike (Sandman) Sanders, Dinada Shields, Colton Skaggs, Aaron Hillard, Alyssa Hines, James Dylan Kneer, Stevie Lockman, Josh Krepp, Josh Burgess(JB), Matt Pun, Roger Crowe, Charlie Bunner, Kenny Kularski(Kizzle), Gary Woodard, Matt Curl, Christopher Isenhour, Melinda Jane McBride, Meghan Watkins

Chapters

Introduction

The fact that I've published this memoir is proof that miracles exist. You see, there was a time when my face was covered in scabs, and my body weighed only 150 lbs. I had been getting high with old dirty needles. It's a memory that still haunts me to this day, but it's also the catalyst for the incredible journey that has brought me to where I am now. Let me take you on a nail biting journey and share with you how I turned my life around.

As a survivor of heroin addiction, I have come to understand the complex and often painful journey that accompanies the struggle to overcome substance abuse. My story is one that I hope will inspire and encourage others who may be facing similar challenges.

It all began when I was just a teenager. I was searching for a way to fit in and be accepted by my peers, and I found solace in drugs and alcohol. At first, getting high/smoking weed was just experimentation. Before I knew it, my drug use had spiraled out of control.

For years, I lived in a fog of addiction. My days were consumed by finding my next fix, and my relationships with loved ones suffered as a result. I tried to quit many times, but I always fell back into old habits. I felt powerless against the pull of my addiction.

It wasn't until I hit rock bottom that I realized I needed help. I had lost everything – my job, my home, and my family and friends. I was alone, desperate, and scared. It was in that moment of despair that I finally found the strength to seek out treatment.

Recovery wasn't easy, but it was worth it. I learned to face my demons head-on and deal with the underlying issues that had led me down the path of addiction. I developed a support system of people who understood what I was going through and who were there to encourage me when things got tough.

I am filled with a sense of gratitude for the people who helped me along the way. My family, my friends, and my counselors were all instrumental in my recovery. They never gave up on me, even when I gave up on myself.

Now, as a survivor of addiction, I want to share my story with others who may be struggling. I want to be a beacon of hope for those who feel trapped by their addiction. I want them to know that recovery is possible and that there is a light at the end of the tunnel.

My memoir is a reflection of my journey, both the highs and the lows. It is a raw and honest account of my struggles with addiction and the challenges that I faced along the way. It is also a tribute to the people who helped me through the darkest moments of my life.

Through my story, I hope to break down the stigma that surrounds addiction and mental health. I want people to understand that addiction is not a moral failing, but rather a complex problem that requires compassion and understanding. I also want to encourage people to seek help when they need it, and to know that they are not alone in their struggles.

Ultimately, my goal is to inspire others to find their own path to recovery. I want them to know that it is possible to live a fulfilling and meaningful life, free from the grips of addiction. I want them to believe that they are worthy of love and happiness, and that they have the strength within themselves to overcome any obstacle.

Through our shared experiences, we can find connection and understanding, and ultimately, heal from the wounds of our past.

I am proud to be a survivor of addiction, and I am grateful for the opportunity to share my story with others. I hope that my memoir will serve as a testament to the resilience of the human spirit and the power of hope in the face of adversity. In writing my memoir, I have come to understand the power of vulnerability and the importance of sharing our stories with one another. It is through our shared experiences that we can find connection and understanding, and ultimately, heal from the wounds of our past.

The Beginning

In the beginning, does anyone know what alcohol and drugs are? As I reflect on my past, I am reminded of how our surroundings shape us into the person we become. For me, that was Evansville, Indiana. My family, in particular, played a significant role in shaping my attitudes toward substance abuse. For instance, on my father's side, not only did his dad drink a case of beer regularly, he had numerous siblings that were drinking every day. He even had one brother who spent a decade in prison for manufacturing methamphetamines.

However, it doesn't stop there. My sister, who recently turned 50, was getting high while babysitting me in the 90s. With all of that going on around me, my parents still worked hard to provide a stable and loving home. I knew that there was a whole world out there that I had yet to discover, and it was through the guidance of those around me that I learned about the harsh realities of addiction.

I remember this weird paradox of being told, this is my family and that I need to steer clear of them because they do bad things. I didn't fully understand what those bad things were until I became a teenager. My earliest memories consist of playing games like Simon Says and Red Light Green Light in our front yard and many other fun things in those first six years of my life.

When I turned six, my parents started to open up and be honest with me about the dangers of drugs and alcohol, and they encouraged me to look at my family members as an attempt at warning me of the consequences of giving in to temptation.

I've mentioned my older sister, who had a house next door, and wasn't the best influence on my younger years. Now is probably the best time to bring up my older brother. My brother is one of the most respected police officers in my hometown. So, as you can see, I wasn't clueless to what was going on in the world outside my parents' house.

As I entered high school, I was exposed to even more outside influences. My health class, in particular, provided a wealth of information about substance abuse and addiction. I vividly remember the stories shared by guest speakers who had lived through the horrors of addiction and the impact those stories had on my curiosity about substance abuse. These cautionary tales mixed with my family dynamics made me want to form my own opinion about substance abuse. Can you blame me? I was hearing how bad it was, and with my eyes I witnessed these family members firsthand, who seemed to be happy. However, my parents and these guest speakers were filling my head up with scary stories.

Looking back, I realize that it was these early life lessons that set me on the path toward a life filled with purpose and fulfillment. They gave me the tools to navigate life's challenges with confidence and strength and instilled in me a deep sense of empathy and compassion for those who are still struggling with addiction.

These experiences I'm about to share with you reinforce the lessons taught by my family and community, and they have strengthened my resolve to lead a life of example.

Life as an Addict

The first time I ever smoked or got high, which was three months before I received my license, was at a church. My sophomore year, I was on the bowling team, and one of the competitors from Central High School and I had an idea to hang out one weekend over Christmas break. We decided it made the most sense to get high and then go bowling afterward. Lucky for me, he was already a stoner, so I didn't have to worry about how to get it. When my parents dropped me off and enough time had passed to where I knew they weren't turning around, we decided to start walking to Diamond Lanes.

Halfway between his house and the alley was this empty church. For whatever reason, we figured that church was the best place to do the deed. I remember asking him what it was called, because I had seen on TV the movie *Friday* with Ice Cube, and I knew weed was more complex than just being weed. He told me it was called Purple Haze. He whipped out a metal bowl that was already packed and his lighter and passed it over to me.

I only remember taking one puff, but it was the biggest breath I had taken up to that point in my life. I was instantly filled with joy and happiness. Everything that came out of my mouth or his seemed to be as funny as a Dave Chapelle routine. It was also one of the only times I can remember being high and not wanting to eat everything in sight. Twenty minutes later, we were at the bowling alley and at the peak of our high.

With what I thought was a straight face, but I'm sure was a grin, I went up to the counter and booked our lane. I believe we only bowled a few frames before I lost all control of myself. The uncontrollable laughter was becoming more noticeable by the second, and I had no idea who was around me. Being dumb, I went up and tried to roll the ball as hard as I possibly could and ended up slipping and falling into the lane. I had a couple friends in the boy scouts who were a few lanes down and they were definitely aware of what was going on.

One of their dads must have called my parents, because next thing I know, I'm answering a phone call in which my mom was screaming as uncontrollably as I was laughing. I knew I was in hot water, so we decided to leave the bowling alley and head back to his house. By the time we got back to his place, my parents had already arrived, and they were waiting for us to walk up. I thanked him for the fun time and hopped into my parents' van. I remember being confused, because my parents were punishing me for something that made me happy to be alive. Little did they know, this was the first of hundreds of crazy high adventures. Little did I know, that would be the beginning of a very long drug addiction. Or, was that the first time I got high?

I'm sure everyone is aware of Adderall and Ritalin. In third grade, my parents thought they were doing the best thing for me by putting me on Metadate CD. They stuck to the doctor's strict regimen of generic stimulant pills that didn't have the same 'addictive' reputation as Adderall. I can't blame them. It worked, and that same week, I went from bad grades and after school detention to straight As and minding my manners while making the honor roll.

My parents also signed me up for basketball, football, and baseball any chance they could, hoping a busy schedule would prevent me from following in the footsteps of my sister and so many others who were in Evansville.

Taking the medication did solve a lot of day-to-day issues I was having, but after I started making good grades and showing respect to the teachers, kids started bullying me. So, in a way, it just replaced my old issues with new ones.

My sophomore year in high school was the "turning point". I earned my driver's license and, because of my new freedom the summer of my sophomore year, I was able to begin finding myself, but before I go on, I want to take a moment to mention a close friend of mine, Ian Duell. May God rest his soul. My good friend, fellow cub scout, and classmate Ian Duell committed suicide on May 14, 2010, ten days before summer break. Ian, me, and our other buddy Tim (my editor) could always be found in English or lunch making the silliest jokes. I had no idea what to think when our teachers told us about his passing. However, I knew I needed to do something, anything, that would help me get back to my happy place. I couldn't find my way back to happiness, and that summer break, smoking weed seemed like as good of an option as any.

After Christmas break, I went back to school and got my license. My buddies Rich, James, Drew, and I met every day to smoke, but that summer, I met Stephen Elkafrawi aka Sparta, who became my best friend from 2010-2016. It was a time in my life that can only be understood if you've seen the movie *Fear and Loathing in Las Vegas*. Sparta is an extremely hard person to describe, and that's a good thing. We tried our hardest to live up to Hunter S. Thompson's words of "Too weird to live, and too rare to die!"

The first time we met was when I was 16 and he was 18, and like usual, I was trying to get some cannabis. He was known around town as the guy who either had the best stuff or knew where to get it. He made life one big Woodstock festival. Over the six-year friendship, we had the pleasure of making hundreds of memories together, but I can only recall a few of them, because of how reckless we had become. Looking back now, I realize we both were only searching for love and acceptance from our peers.

Our life became the same underground movement that began in the late sixties with Jimi and

Dylan and more specifically the Grateful Dead. I was 16 when I tried mushrooms, and 17 when I tripped on acid for the first time. Sparta was "my brother from another mother" as we used to say, who showed me a world I never knew existed. Electric Forest, Bonnaroo, and Wakarusa are some festivals we went to from when I was 17-21, and it got to the point where we lost count of the number of festivals, and I can't remember how many raves over the years. One Halloween, we went to a rave that was in a St. Louis cave if you can believe it. We made it a priority to hit the road and follow the music. Drugs, more specifically psychedelics, became a daily part of our lives at a really young age.

Because we went to all of these festivals that were similar to Woodstock, we had connections, which meant everyone wanted us at their parties. We always brought mushrooms, molly, weed, and LSD wherever we went. It was totally normal for us to wake up on a Thursday morning and figure out how many parties we were going to in the next three days.

When junior year of school began in August 2010, Sparta and I were hanging out every single day. It's hard not to recall the electrifying thrill that came with my introduction to the core friends, the infamous Bear, Milkman, Regan, and Sarah Foley. You see, Sparta introduced me to every one of my childhood friends that are still around today and the ones who aren't.

I ended up getting expelled from Castle High School May 13, 2011 for smoking weed in the school parking lot before school, and that is my first memory of getting in serious trouble. Because of my excessive smoking and partying and getting expelled, I had to take a few classes over my junior/senior year summer.

It was May 2011, roughly about two weeks before the last day of school. I was meeting my buddy and his girlfriend before school started like always when they showed up and hopped in my car with some cannabis. We started hotboxing his car like always in the parking lot across from the school. We were getting close to finishing when the school sheriff and the vice principal showed up.

They got us out of the car and started interrogating us on what we were doing in the car. The three of us denied everything, so they took us into the principal's office one by one. When it was my turn, which was last, they had already gotten all of the information they needed to expel us. The vice principal had my mom come in as well. To my surprise, they weren't failing any of us. Instead, they decided to give us a free pass to our senior year. The catch was if we had any failing grades, we didn't receive an opportunity to raise them.

It was the start of finals week, and they just wanted us out of there. Lucky for me, there was one class I was failing, which meant I was getting an early summer and only had to make up one English class. That was the first of my two expulsions. The second one was during my first semester of my senior year in the month of November. When I was done with the court cases after being arrested and put on house arrest until I graduated, I went back to Castle High School, where the principals expelled me once again, but this time it was for truancy or commonly known as too many absences.

Little did I know, one summer school day would mark the beginning of a heart-pumping adventure that would forever change my life. My phone lit up with a text from Sparta, and my heart raced as I read the message. Bear was coming down from Indy and wanted to know if we needed any favors. I was intrigued, but Sparta's proposition to pool our money for a bigger and better deal had me on the edge of my seat. It was a gamble, but the possibility of a high reward was too tempting to resist.

I brought up the question, *What would we get?* To my surprise, he brought to my attention Molly. I had heard it was like ecstasy, but I hadn't tried it yet. I found out years later that Sparta had been lying to me all along, and that he was completely broke.

Anyway, it was too late, my adrenaline was already pumping, and my mind was set on this risky venture. I knew I had to get my hands on some cash, and I convinced myself that taking my dad's stash was the only option. The fear and excitement were indescribable as we embarked on this wild ride of deceit and danger, all in the name of adventure! The deciding factor in me taking my dad's money was when I convinced myself we would only do the profits and would sell the rest to return the money before he found out. More on that later…

This was the first time I would meet Bear, or so I thought. Up to this point, Milkman, Sarah, and Regan were the crew. Sparta had an elaborate explanation of why I needed to stand watch in the parking lot of his apartments. Off to my Camry I went, and before I knew it, he called me to come back upstairs. My jaw dropped when he showed me the bag! I'd say it was close to two ounces if not more.

I ended up actually meeting Bear outside of Milkman's apartment a week or so later. Milkman was living in a towering apartment down by the Ohio River. The neighboring apartment was vacant with the door unlocked. Milkman would invite Sparta and I over weekly to chill and smoke in that vacant apartment, and we even threw a couple acid tests in there for about three months until the managers rented it out.

Another great memory from that summer came from another text asking me to come over. I met up with Sparta to figure out what we were going to do for Friday night, and he told us it was Sarah's twenty-first, and she had rented out Club Icon. So, we did what we did best and opened the safe and pulled out seven grams of Molly and started bagging it up. We set aside three grams as a present for Sarah, one for each of us, and two to sell to others, in an attempt to make our money back on Sarah's gift and do ours for free. The club was 18 and up, so I whipped out my fake ID and made it past the bouncer. Everyone came up to me like a pack of hyenas questioning where the drugs were, including people we had never met before, so I turned around and ran back to the apartment to grab another three grams. Sparta and I divided two grams between us and the crew and ended up giving the last gram away to Sarah's friends so she wouldn't have to share her present. A couple hours into the roll, Xybrium breaks his foot running back and forth between the stage and the VIP lounge.

With the party being over, everyone was high and looking for a place to go. Someone stepped up and said they had a pool and their parents were out of town. Twenty of us hopped into cars to rush to his place so we could resume our partying.

Regan, Sparta, and I got there, and everyone had already started hopping into the hot tub and pool. Someone we knew pulled out some gold cap mushrooms and asked us if we wanted to go on a trip. Everyone smiled and put out their hands. An hour into being at this random guy's house, I found these glow sticks tied to shoe strings and was immediately drawn to them. I picked them up and started spinning and the lights were mesmerizing. In a blink of an eye, the sun was coming up, and we were all being asked to leave. Sparta, Regan, and I headed down to our normal chill spot at the Ohio River to smoke a blunt and watch the sunrise while the visuals wore off.

Sometime in the following days, I received an urgent voicemail from Sparta. It said, I had to ditch summer school right then and pick him up. Of course, I called back and asked him why, and he told me one of our great friends Nessa needed our help, because she was stranded ninety miles away in Louisville and needed to be rescued and brought back to Evansville. I instantly ran out of the house to my car, and off we went on this road trip. We got to Louisville and ran out of gas down the street from where Nessa was hanging out. We filled up by over drafting my bank account and went straight home. She gave me gas money to replenish my account. After the long drive back, we dropped her off and then went back to his place to call it a night.

The partying didn't stop though. In fact, it had gotten worse. For instance, the first time I personally smoked meth was this same year. When you live young and reckless, you are bound to make serious mistakes, and that's exactly what happened that night.

Dinada lived on the same street and she had helped me get weed numerous times. I was actually looking for weed that night as well, but Sparta was nowhere to be found at midnight. She told me to come over and she would call her people. Turned out, nobody had weed but they had meth, and I was dying to get high. I was wanting to escape so badly I decided what the heck! Remember, I took generic Adderall, so in my brain, I was simply staying within the realm of stimulants. The thought "If cannabis and psychedelics were fun and helped my mental state, maybe everyone was lying about meth and other drugs as well" was my demise.

Dinada told me we had to go get it because of how late it was. I will never forget walking into that broke down place to find Sparta in the kitchen. We both looked like we had seen a ghost. After we collected ourselves, I remember feeling this sense of comfort. Which, of course, made me feel more comfortable with going through with it.

He called me over to the countertop where I saw some powder and a glass pipe. He opened the drawer and pulled out this tiny torch and he proceeded to make the one end of the glass pipe red hot. Sparta passed it over to me and said, "Here, stick that end up your nose and snort this." I instantly blew out a huge cloud of smoke and felt this rushing tingling sensation consume my head. The rest of the night is foggy, but seeing as I'm alive today, it's not that important.

Nearing the end of summer in 2011, my friends Sparta, Regan, and I embarked on an exciting journey to Louisville. Our purpose was to reunite with our buddies Swazay and Jumbie, who were attending the University of Louisville. Arriving at their home, we ventured into their basement, a vibrant sanctuary adorned with a pool table and Jumbie's captivating psychedelic artwork adorning the walls.

Eagerly, we delved into the experience, indulging in nitrous balloons that heightened our senses. Mesmerized by Jumbie's remarkable creations, we found ourselves lost in a sea of colors and patterns.

However, as the night unfolded, Regan pushed her limits and succumbed to the effects. Her head collided with the pool table, triggering slight seizures, a phenomenon known as phishing out, which was a completely new and alarming experience for me.

The atmosphere shifted, and it became evident that the lively gathering had come to an abrupt end. We bid farewell to our friends and embarked on the journey back to Evansville, with memories and lessons from that eventful night etched in our minds forever.

The first festival that I ever snuck into was Tall Tree Music Fest September 2011. I was with a group of friends, and they asked if I could get any shrooms, because we wanted to go camping. I sent Sparta a text to see what he was up to, and he said he was in Goreville, Illinois at this fest. I looked it up, and it was three hours away, so I hopped in the car with two of my friends and hit the road. Little did I know, this would be my first time seeing Leftover Salmon.

We got there late Friday night, and the gatekeepers told us it was fifty-five bucks each for the three of us, and we only had 100 bucks. So, needless to say, we turned around and drove down the road to the other side of the forest and snuck in. Once we walked through the half-mile of woods, I called Sparta and found where he was camping. On the way to find him, I found a kid I went to school with who was also around the scene a lot and my really good friend Cody Ward. Before I found Sparta, we stopped at Cody's campsite, where my classmate actually had some really powerful gold caps.

The three of us got 3.5 grams each and ate them right there in front of the fire. About this time, Sparta came rolling through the campsite carrying a two-foot tall nitrous tank and almost passed right by me until I grabbed his arm. We ended up not needing to go search for him, but that's not surprising, because Sparta was always running around meeting new people. We ended up splitting up shortly after that and headed to go see Leftover Salmon while the shrooms slowly kicked in.

While we were at the stage, my buddy got a call from his mom, and she was extremely upset with him that we left the state to go to a party. At this point, the shrooms were starting to get intense and wildly vivid, and I could tell we had about forty-five minutes before we peaked. I asked him what he wanted to do. He said we had to go back to town, so we left the barn and headed back for the woods. We needed my good friend Cody to guide us there, because we were fully hallucinating at this point. Walking through the woods was an experience all on its own.

All of the trees seemed so symmetrical for example. They were extremely tall and all in a perfect line. They seemed like they went on forever and ever, and we started to get anxious that we would be walking around until the sun came up. Luckily, we were just tripping and found our way out of the woods thirty minutes later. I'm not really sure why I let my buddy Abe take my keys, but it was a horrible idea, since he had never tripped before let alone drove while tripping. We were driving for what felt like days, but in reality, it was only an hour into the drive when Abe started to wig out.

He started speaking gibberish and would look over at me like he was expecting me to respond in his same alien language. Our other friend in the backseat started to panic as well since his trip was connected to all of ours. I was able to convince Abe to pull over on the side of the road. When we got out of the car to switch seats, Abe walked out on the highway. I saw two lights in the distance and immediately ran over to Abe and grabbed him. Then, I dragged him out of the road and put him in the passenger seat.

I locked the door and ran over to the driver's side and hopped in. I had put the GPS coordinates in my Garmin before we left, and I think without doing that we could've ended up in serious trouble. I remember driving down the highway looking at the exit signs as my headlights shined in the dark. I kept seeing the same exit signs over and over, and eventually, I started to believe I was caught in a time loop. My anxiety started to build as I was unsure if the time loop would ever end. My Garmin, of course, was telling me when and where to turn, so luckily, at 6 a.m., we rolled back into the campsite. We all slung the doors open, leaned out, and puked simultaneously, and then the trip was over as we sat back into our car seats.

After that, Abe and I didn't see or speak to each other. We used to skip class every week together to smoke and dream about our future lives, and after that night, we just drifted apart. There were times when Sparta and I would take a few days off from seeing each other. Mostly because we never knew how to stop the party, and we would just need to rest or our bodies felt like they were giving up.

During another week-long bender, I was bouncing around hotels, hanging out with a few people including Lexxie, a girl two grades ahead of me at Castle, who later on reconnected with me through heroin, rented this car for us to use. One day, Tay and Jay, our close friends, had invited us to this house party, and next thing I know, Tay and I were doing a line of bath salts with Lexxie. The party bounced around to a different house or hotel each night until one night I got arrested.

It was a very cold winter, and I had been away from home for a while at this point, and I decided it would be a good time to go home. What I didn't know was that during my bender my Dad had noticed the money from my summer escapades was missing. After I fell asleep, my parents called the cops, and I woke up in the middle of the night to a cop walking down the hall and arresting me. I didn't know it at the time, but that night would forever change my life, and it was also my first time going to jail.

The cop took me to the county juvenile hall where I had to stay the weekend until the judge was in on Monday. When I went to court, my parents were there to meet me outside the courtroom. They called everyone in. The judge came out, and we all stood. He asked the state prosecutors to read out the charges.

The first one was a misdemeanor for running away, the second was for stealing a laptop out of a pawn shop, and the third was for being in possession of a stolen rental car. The judge turned to my family and me and asked my dad to speak. He told the judge I was a smart kid. That I had become mixed up with the wrong crowd, and that since I was really close to finishing high school, he hoped the judge would find a way to give me another chance. He looked back at the prosecutors and asked what they thought. I was stunned when I heard them say they wanted to charge me as an adult and send me to Indiana Corrections for four years.

Because I was a minor, the judge had my parents in there next to me. I tried to remain tough and hard, but inside, I couldn't breathe. For some reason, the judge had come to a decision pretty quickly after speaking to my parents. The judge decided that instead of sending me to prison as an adult, I should be put on house arrest and reporting probation until I graduated high school. They even made a deal to expunge my record if I went into the military, which I did in June 2012.

I felt so grateful the judge showed me mercy and didn't send me to prison at seventeen. I knew this meant I had to play by the rules by getting my diploma, passing my drug tests, and leaving for basic training, but before I threw my childhood away completely, I wanted to enjoy my last days as a child. Which is why after I graduated and before I left for basic training in San Antonio, Sparta and I planned a trip to Bonnaroo.

My trip to Bonnaroo was in June 2012, and I was about to go to basic training for the Air Force in San Antonio in two weeks, like the great Chuck Norris and amazing Morgan Freeman before me. I had recently graduated from Castle High School with a diploma. My parents didn't know if I was going to graduate since I was expelled my junior and senior year. Bonnaroo was my last hurrah before having to 'grow up.' My best friend Sparta and I had been going to music festivals for the last six months at this point, but Bonnaroo with the 100,000 people was certainly the biggest one yet.

Up until then, we typically got in for free, because we knew everyone and everyone knew we had everything, such as nitrous, Molly, tabs, triple stacks, whippets, magic mushrooms, ketamine, and other various substances depending on the time of year. You see, we were very familiar with bitcoin and using the silk road to find what we needed. To our peers, we were like Scarface, but to our best friends Bear and Milkman, we were just two nerds trying to be tough cool hippies. Sparta was dating his baby mama at the time. We all went to Castle and were all in different grades.

Sparta was supposed to graduate in 2010, his baby mama graduated in 2011, and I in 2012. His baby mama didn't have as big of a free spirit attitude as we did at this point, but she certainly caught up. So, Sparta and I packed up my car once again and headed three hours south to Manchester, Tennessee. On the way out of town, my homie Dman called. I always picked up his call, since he was the only guy I knew crazy enough to say yes to every idea I had. He filled me in on a big fight he had just went through with his family and how they kicked him out since he was eighteen. The tickets to Bonnaroo cost $300 each, and I had only pre-bought two tickets. Oddly enough, my mom gave me 300 bucks to make sure I wasn't ill-prepared . So, I made a U turn and picked up Dman.

We got into the car line at the entrance of Bonnaroo at sun fall the day before the music started, and man, were there already tens of thousands of people. We got to the front of the line around 2 a.m. and spent every penny on Dman's ticket. By the time we got to our campsite, it was Thursday morning, and the sun was starting to rise. Luckily, Sparta and I had a screw it attitude and only brought drugs and alcohol, so setting up the campsite took no time. We only had a canopy and chairs with sleeping bags.

No tent, no food, and no water. Just clothes and a good attitude. Bonnaroo had some amazing artists, and it was the first time I had the opportunity to see the Beach Boys, Alice Cooper, Skrillex, Major Lazer, Mimosa, Big Gigantic and many more artists.

Sparta's baby mama got jealous once she found out how much fun we were having and showed up on Saturday. By this time, Dman, Sparta, and I had been tripping for days, and we had been rolling for days. We hadn't been eating either, and the last thing we wanted to do was orchestrate a plan, but we weren't going to let her be stuck outside the gates, so Dman slid off his wristband, then Sparta and I snuck outside the gates, met her to give her the ticket, and then, with our tickets, we entered into the festival.

The festival was set to end on Monday, so we figured she would stay the entire trip, but after Saturday night and then a crazy day Sunday, she forced Sparta to leave a day early, leaving Drew and me behind with $15, an eighth of a gas tank, and no cigarettes.

Our neighbors however were super cool, and they invited us to join their group for the very last day on Monday, and since we were broke, I figured why not just ask somebody for free drugs, and eventually, one person had to be high enough to give it to us, and I was right. After about eight people, this Jamaican dread headed homie had walked by, and I decided to shout

out to him and ask if he had a free trip. Crazy enough, he did, and everyone including me was surprised.

He pulled out a ten strip, and we each took two hits till it was gone. This was right before Brian Wilson and the Beach Boys came on, and then, after they left, the trip was in full force. Phish was the headliner, and boy did they blow our minds. This was the first time I experienced the glow stick wars. I can't lie, it is the only thing I vividly remember about the festival even though we were there for five whole days, met thousands and thousands of people. We even gave hugs to complete strangers, but I can't remember those experiences remotely close to the experience of watching thousands of glow sticks being thrown up into the pitch-black sky.

Until this point, Sparta had made music festivals strictly about business. It was about networking with customers, getting their cell phone number as long as I lived within a two-hour radius, and then after the festival making sure they wanted stuff brought to their town. Something about watching The Beach Boys and then Phish on hallucinogens reset my brain. It was as he would call pulling the power switch. When we woke up the next morning and headed back down, our neighbors gave us $20 for gas, which in my Camry got us all the way home.

Now that I had experienced Bonnaroo, I could gladly leave for basic training. What I didn't know, however, was that my time spent in the Air Force would be another rude awakening and life lesson. Of course, I was expecting basic training to be challenging, both mentally and physically. What I wasn't prepared for, however, was all of the politics inside the branch.

Being in the Air Force felt much like another high school. I quickly learned that you couldn't truly open up to anyone or you would risk them using it against you later on down the road. I didn't even make it out of basic training before a scandal happened. It wasn't my training squad but our neighboring airman. A drill sergeant was trading sexual favors with his female trainees for special privileges like alcohol, tobacco, and extra phone time, all of which were extremely forbidden.

He wasn't the only instructor abusing his position of power, though. The biggest scandal while I was in basic training was the one about our laundry room on base. An instructor was caught forcing airmen in training to perform sexual acts on him in the laundry room. During one of these occasions, another airman from a different squadron walked in on the instructor while he was raping his airman. Once this news got out, it spread like wildfire, and it wasn't long before the entire base knew about what was happening.

The general on the base at the time had to do something, but it was what he said that made me realize I was just a high paid slave in the eyes of the government. When the next morning came around and it was time to hear the daily announcements, the only thing the general said was that he was aware how everyone knew about the horrible things going on and that we didn't have to worry, that the instructor would be facing a court martial and serious jail time, but we were forbidden from calling home and telling anyone about it. The general even said if anyone was caught leaking the news to a civilian source, they would be in as much trouble as the instructor.

I only had a couple more weeks left until I graduated basic training, so unfortunately, I pretended like I didn't know anything and just kept my head down until I could move onto my next duty station. Before I knew it, September 2012 was here, and it was graduation time. Graduating basic training was more exciting than graduating high school. My parents, grandparents, and my brother's family all came out to watch it happen. Afterward, I found out my next station was Keesler AFB in Biloxi, Mississippi.

Our instructors gave us three days to visit with our families before shipping out. We went to see the Alamo and the San Antonio Riverwalk, and both were breathtaking in their own ways. When I got to Keesler that following Monday, I felt like I had entered college. The sole purpose of me being there was to go to school and to learn how to be an electrical engineer for the Air Force. Our instructors now called us airmen in training, and the way they assigned our barracks, or as I called them our dorms, was based on our careers.

They had us all line up and called out our names and which dorms we were assigned. It made it easier for them to march us in between our dorm and classes as well as to do physical training. It didn't take long for me to make friends. In the military, they had designated smoking sections, so everyone would take smoke breaks, goof around, and come up with plans for the weekend. At Keesler, every other week was a four-day work week, which meant every other week was a big party because it was an hour from New Orleans and an hour and a half from Pensacola, Florida. Biloxi is also known as the Vegas of the Gulf, but since I was only 18, the casinos didn't interest me.

Another interesting fact about Keesler in 2012 was that it ranked #2 as having the most airmen with STDs out of every Air Force Base. Now, I don't know if it's still running rampant with STDs, but it gives you an idea of the partying that was going on.

Most weekends, my buddy Chaz, Monty, and I would pitch in to book a penthouse suite at the beach hotel in Biloxi, and we would have about 30-40 people raging the night away. There is one penthouse party in particular that I will never forget. It was the party where Monty and I made our killer Jungle Juice. We put everything from Everclear to Coors Banquet and even some Red Bull for energy. We made the juice in those five-gallon igloo jugs that you see on the sidelines at football games.

It only took everyone drinking two red solo cups to start chanting UFC. Next thing I knew, Chaz and Monty were moving all of the living room furniture into the master bedroom, so we could turn the living room into the Octagon. The guys had all started chatting about who was going to fight who. The girls being the level headed ones reminded us that if anyone got seriously hurt our superior officers would most likely court martial us. After taking that into consideration, we decided to make it a tap out match and that no hitting or kicking was allowed.

Naturally, since there were about twenty gorgeous women at the party, I agreed to wrestle Monty, but I wanted us to go last. While the three matches before ours were going on, I took the opportunity to smoke a cig with Chaz. He called me out to the deck to talk about a girl he had been hitting it off with. It was Monty and my turn before I knew it. I guess it wasn't taking long for people to tap out.

Monty got everyone to be quiet and figured it would be a great time to let everyone know that he had become divisional champ in wrestling in Santa Maria his senior year, which was literally 7-8 months ago at this time. When the match started, we both hugged each other like two boxers. I swung my right leg on the inside of his left leg and used my left leg to push and make him trip and fall backward. After what Monty had told the entire party, they looked surprised and gasped when I took him down. However, Monty didn't let that little maneuver throw his game off.

He quickly reversed me onto my back and was trying to put me in a choke hold. After a few minutes, he was able to get the hold locked in and was looking to the crowd to start chanting "TAP". Little did they know, I black out before I tap out, and this situation wasn't any different. I whispered in Monty's ear to kiss my ass, and in a flash, I was waking up to everyone standing over me. I didn't realize it at first, but I ended up peeing my pants when he choked me out, and that caused the entire party to question if I was going to be okay or not and if they needed to call for help.

I was embarrassed by the outcome to say the least, so I quickly hopped up off the ground and shouted to everyone to refill their drinks, and my buddy Chaz turned back on the surround sound music. Because my ego was bruised, I decided that a few more cups of Jungle Juice would ease the pain. It wasn't very long before I lost all control of my motor functions. In total, I blacked out after four cups of Jungle Juice. The next morning when I came to, I was oddly stuck in between the corner of the pull-out couch mattress and the metal frame. Chaz helped me get unstuck, and we had the place back to brand new in two hours, and nobody from the hotel staff said a thing about loud noises or a trashed room when we checked out at noon.

Halloween 2012 was the time Chaz and I had a great idea to go to Bourbon Street, since our base was so close. I was 18 and asked him how I would get alcohol and wouldn't there be cops patrolling. He said not to worry, since he went to college in New Orleans and was friends with a few club managers, and we wouldn't be in the streets except to go from place to place, and the cops have bigger issues to worry about. We got together with a couple of girls, Kenz and June, and off to the liquor store we went. We bought a fifth of Jack Daniels and a two-liter of cherry coke that way we could pre-game on our hour-long drive we had.

Once we got off the base, we cracked open the bottle and started passing her around. About twenty minutes into the drive, Kenz asked if anyone wanted to look for some coke while we were there. Chaz spoke right up and mentioned he had a buddy who sold some that could have it ready when we got there. I asked him how much 3.5 grams usually cost since there were four of us, and he said about $150. To me, that sounded like a great deal, so I told him to put in the order and to have his buddy leave it in his mailbox, so we could just swing by to grab it and leave behind the cash.

As promised, it was there waiting in his buddy's mailbox when we showed up twenty minutes later, and once we had it, we flew over to his other friends' house who was letting the four of us stay there after we were done partying. By this time, it was 5:30, and the sun was setting. We all rushed to get our costumes on. Kenz and June went as Mario and Luigi, and Chaz and I brought our Air Force uniforms, because we didn't plan ahead for Halloween. I also figured it might help me with the cops if I got caught and it might win me a free drink or two from a grateful citizen.

While Chaz and I waited on the girls to get ready, we broke up our baggie and plopped down a line for each of us to try. This was the first time in my life I came across coke, and as far as first experiences go, I believe I had one of the best ones in history. I was already on the verge of being drunk when we got there, and doing the line instantly brought me back to normal or so my mind felt. The girls came out of the bathroom and asked for some. While Chaz prepared it for them, I decided to line up four more shots of whiskey.

Down the hatch it all went and out the door we went. It was seven o' clock, and it was time to go party on Bourbon Street. We were very lucky that Chaz had a friend that lived within walking distance, because none of us were able to drive and were planning on certainly forgetting how to drive by the end of the night. As soon as we got on the strip, out from the first bar comes running this woman in a tight eighties workout suit. She was very attractive, and she was calling me over, so off I went.

Chaz started laughing and whispering, but I didn't pay any attention to it. When we got back to the bar, she pulled out these test tubes that were filled with all different bright colors. She lifted up my shirt and slid the first tube into my boxers. Then she bent over and grabbed it out with her mouth and took it with no hands. Out came another tube, and this time, she slid it down into her cleavage and told me to take it.

While I was grabbing the shot out with my mouth, she started shaking her chest. I couldn't believe what was happening right now, and I thought I was the coolest eighteen-year-old alive until she asked me for $40. I thought I misunderstood and asked her to repeat herself, and she told me the shots were $20 each and asked if I wanted more. I politely declined and gave her a crisp $50. I looked to see where the rest of the group was, and I found them in the corner laughing uncontrollably.

Now, I realized what the joke was and how they all knew I was falling into a trap. My spirits were down, so Chaz offered to go into the bathroom so we could sneak a few bumps, and I couldn't resist. June and Kenz had made friends with a little person dressed up as a leprechaun and had bought a round of shots for the three of them to do. When Chaz and I got back and found them with a leprechaun, we asked if they wanted another round of shots, which, of course, they said yes to. After the shots, we had a stranger take our photo, so we could remember the night.

To this day, I never saw the photo or even knew which person's phone it was taken on. Now that it was a little after 8, Bourbon street had started to get packed and it was almost elbow to elbow, not only in the bars, but even the street. Chaz brought up the famous hand grenade drink, which I hadn't heard of. I asked him what was in it, and he said all the good stuff and laughed, then proceeded to tell me it had gin, vodka, rum, and melon liqueur. It sounded tasty to me, and he pointed to someone in the crowd holding this long green plastic tube with a hand grenade at the bottom.

I thought it was the coolest souvenir and asked him to take us to get one. When we got there, the bar had a separate line for the hand grenades, and it was twenty people long. I didn't realize how much of a significant drink it was, and when we got to the front of the line, our buzzes had started to wear off. Chaz and I grabbed two each and headed to find Kenz and June. They had stumbled into a nightclub with a DJ and made us come to them.

As soon as we found them, we handed off their drinks and rushed to the bathroom to do some more bumps. When we came out, the girls were on the dance floor, so we decided to join them. We stayed there dancing, grabbing shots, and using the restroom until there became a waiting line at the bar and bathroom. Nobody knew what time it was at this point, but we did know that we were getting very hungry. Chaz knew this great hole in the wall that served deep fried chicken, and as twisted as we were, that sounded like the perfect meal.

It took a few minutes to swim through the crowd and get to the place, but when we did, the smell was so delicious it made our stomachs jump. The girls ran inside to get in line, and Chaz and I stayed in the street to smoke a cigarette. By the time we finished our cigarettes, the girls had come outside with the food. We all grabbed a piece and ripped into it when these three girls came running up on us shouting curse words. All of us were startled and had trouble finding words.

Finally, June was able to ask them what their problem was. Quickly, they fired back with how June and Kenz stole their order. Really confused, Kenz spoke up and said there's no way their order was stolen and that they grabbed what we had ordered. One of the three girls ran inside and asked the cashier if Kenz and June had the right order. The cashier leaned over the counter to see Kenz and said her order wasn't ready yet and that they had happened to order the same thing as the other girls and mistakenly grabbed it when they saw it had everything they ordered.

The girl came running back out and got in Kenz's face while the other two girls were shouting in June's face. Kenz got mad that this girl was in her face and decided it was a good idea to tell them to screw off and that their food tasted even better now that she knew it was stolen. That was a horrible idea, because the girl swung a right hook and landed it right on Kenz's chin, and her head flew back and hit the brick wall. Her Ray Ban sunglasses went flying off ,and June swung on the other two girls. Chaz and I looked at each other like this was really happening, and we turned back to watch the fight.

While June knocked down one girl with an uppercut, she grabbed the second girl and started pulling her weave out. All the while, Kenz is getting hit over and over by the one girl. I look over and see a mounted cop bobbing and weaving through the crowd.

I shouted to the girls, and the fight instantly stopped, and off we all went running in opposite directions. Chaz led me and the girls into a crowded club, so we could regroup and figure out what just happened, but first, we rushed to the bathroom for some more bumps.

We got into the men's room and saw an empty stall. We were so shaken up that we spilled some onto the floor. The girls were also shaken up and just wanted a drink to calm down. June jokingly asked what happened to Kenz since she was able to take out two girls, and Kenz couldn't even handle one. That was just what the group needed to have the tension go away, so we could get back to having a good time. We decided it was a good place to finish the night off with and didn't leave until all of the coke was gone except enough to get us through the next morning.

While we were stumbling out of the bar, we saw this woman passed out sitting on the ground in this corner. We didn't know if she was okay or even alive, so we flagged down a horse cop, and when he came over and shouted at the woman, she magically sprang to life and hopped up. When the cop asked if she was on anything, she took off running from the cop. The crowd was still so thick that he couldn't chase after this crazy woman. Chaz looked over and said on that note, let's go home, and everyone let out a gut-wrenching laugh, because we didn't think this night could get any crazier, and now, we didn't want to stay out to see what else would happen. As soon as we got back to our friends' place, we fell right to sleep.

The next morning came, and I was the first one up as usual. I went on the balcony to smoke a cigarette, and my mouth had this nasty taste like vomit, but I knew I hadn't thrown up. Luckily, the cigarette killed the taste, and before I knew it, Chaz came out. He mentioned having a similar taste, and when I said I had the same thing, he said it was because of all the coke we snorted the night before. About an hour later, Kenz and June woke up, and they looked even worse than we did.

Kenz had a swollen lip, but June just looked like she was left outside in the rain. We all agreed that we were starving, and Chaz suggested that we go to Café du Monde in the French Quarter to get some world-famous beignets. Not sure what they were but wanting to embrace the culture, I offered to pay for everyone. We got our food and scarfed it down, so we could get back on the road to Biloxi, Mississippi.

A couple weeks later, I got a notice that I was being relocated to Sheppard Air Force base in Wichita Falls, Texas. Chaz ended up spending a year in federal prison for getting caught with ecstasy, and as far as Monty, Kenz, and June, I lost contact and have no clue where they are today, but I hope it's someplace as nice as where God has brought me.

The job I had in the military of working on the parts of a B1 bomber had two parts of school. I didn't know this when I first graduated basic training, but the second part of my airmen job training was in Wichita Falls, Texas, and we had to get there before Thanksgiving hit. I had made some real friends outside of my hippie friends, so I was extremely sad, but there was nothing I was allowed to do besides get over it and get on the bus for my twelve-hour ride.

When our bus finally arrived at Sheppard AFB, it was three in the morning, and we were all sleeping. That was until the staff sergeant came running aboard, screaming and shouting for everyone to "get your sorry asses up and off this fucking pathetic excuse for a bus." A faint whisper started to fill the air between us young airmen, and if you listened closely, you would've heard it saying, "Who the hell is this guy and doesn't he know basic training ended two months ago?"

As we were stumbling off the bus in our undone pants and unlaced boots, there were two other sergeants waiting to form us in a single file line. They weren't shouting like the first one, which was a relief.

Once all fifty-two airmen were off the bus, we marched inside our headquarters to get our roommate and room number assignments. I ended up getting a room on the second out of four floors, thank goodness. When Obama was in office in 2012, he removed the don't ask don't tell policy, which in turn allowed everyone to be who they truly wanted to be, but in my case, my roommate was under the impression that it meant he should tell everyone he sees. I could have cared less when he told me that first night, but I did let him know we would have issues if he didn't respect my personal space.

He assured me that he was on the night shift and for the last two months until his graduation we would only see each other in passing. As I mentioned earlier, during basic training young men were getting sexually abused by their gay drill sergeants, so the thought of having to defend myself was certainly in the back of my head.

I will let you know now that my roommate was an amazing person and the few encounters we had after that first one were all about our goals in the military and what we wanted to accomplish in life, which was really comforting at times, since your roommate is the only person who you can talk to that understands what you're going through.

I found Sheppard AFB to be the exact opposite of my time at Kessler in Biloxi, Mississippi. For starters, our work week went from four days back to five, and our leaders in charge went from being mentors who guided and helped us into angry leaders who only treated us like they were waiting for us to screw up, so they could punish us. Nonetheless, I was able to make friends with a guy named Lars, who was a couple weeks ahead of me in training.

We connected on the fact that we were both from the Midwest, and in fact, he was from St. Louis, which is only a few hours away from Evansville, so it just felt like we should be friends. Since he had been there a couple weeks already, he knew of the bars to go to that weren't full of other military. However, we wouldn't always leave the base on a Friday or Saturday night, because the base had bars and designated areas for drinking and smoking.

One of the times we stayed on the base in December, Lars met Jenny from the block, this short but full of attitude girl from Rhode Island who loved to drink and party as much as we did. The three of us would go out line dancing, and I'd end up spending two to three hundred dollars on shots of tequila. Because of our society and how young men were raised, I thought being in the military made me a man, which should mean I could drink like a man...

But in reality, I was still the eighteen-year-old teenager who just six months prior graduated high school and got off house arrest. There were many times when I blacked out only to wake up in a pile of vomit, missing my car keys and wallet. Even though it had happened several times, at the time, I told myself, I was having fun and this was what made people like me so much. I'll tell you now that couldn't have been further from the truth... but we aren't to that part of the story yet. You see, it's Christmas time, and Sheppard let everyone go home for seven days to see family and friends.

When I got the news, I was so excited, I rushed upstairs to my room to call my parents and let them know I'd be there to decorate the tree. My next phone calls were to Sparta and Drew to let them know I wanted to see my best friends. When I landed at the Evansville airport, I felt a huge sense of relief to be back home. My mom was, too, with how big of a hug she gave me.

I spent the first four days solely visiting with my family, but after Christmas Day was over, I wanted to see my friends. I had to be back at Sheppard January 2, so there wasn't too much time to see everyone I used to party with, so I spent it with just Sparta and Drew. They both had their own apartments, and we could easily party and not worry. Before I knew it, my time at home was over, and my parents were dropping me back off at the airport.

There was definitely sadness in the air, and every bone in my body wished I didn't have to go back. It wasn't that I wanted out of the military, but that I had wished my actions as a seventeen-year-old hadn't driven me so far from home and everything I was comfortable with. Nevertheless, I had to bury my feelings and return to my new life. Everyone I talked to seemed to be upset we were back on base.

We figured it was smart to go out and forget about having to leave home. As usual, it was Jenny, Lars, and me out at the line dancing bar. Except something happened that night that never happened before.

Jenny leaned over to Lars and me and asked if we had ever smoked pot before. Lars and I looked at each other confused, he asked her why she wanted to know. Jenny told us she didn't leave the base over Christmas break, and instead, stayed behind and threw a big party for everyone else who stayed back. At this party, a handful of airmen were underage. One of them being a female that was sexually assaulted by a male, who was also drunk underage, and when the female went to the office of special investigations and told them what had happened, OSI went straight to Jenny and arrested her for facilitating underage drinking at her party.

She then mentioned she asked because she just wanted to smoke some pot and forget about everything that happened. I thought that was very understandable, so I admitted I used to smoke before joining, and Lars admitted it as well. I went on to say I hadn't done it since and had no clue where to get any in Texas. She asked Lars and me if we would be open to helping her find some, and drunk me being the helping type said sure why not, but I wasn't going to smoke with her because of the random drug tests we were subjected to.

Since we were at a bar, I decided to walk up to the closest bartender and ask them if they could help me out with a favor. When they heard I was looking to score some pot, they were kind of taken aback, because they could tell I was in the Air Force. I assured them I was cool and wasn't an undercover cop, and they gave me their phone number and told me they were off at 3 a.m. I went back to the table with Lars and Jenny and told her the good news and gave her the number. She seemed excited but asked if Lars and I would go with her, so she wouldn't get robbed or something more serious.

We said sure while thinking can you be serious, and before we knew it, we were at the bartender's house, buying an eighth off of them. When Jenny came back to the car, she asked if we wanted to go get a hotel room and hang out with her while she smoked. Being as we were super drunk and didn't want to go back to base, we thought she had a good idea. When we got the room at the local Best Western, she asked if one of us could roll a joint for her, and Lars rolled a nice Pearl for her. We went on the deck to smoke cigs while she smoked and off to bed it was.

The next day, we stumbled back onto base like the night before never happened and back into the military routine it was. The next weekend rolled around, and Jenny didn't want to go out, but Lars did, and this time, he wanted to smoke when he got drunk. Next thing I knew, off to the guy's house we went, and we were debating whether we should smoke or not, and I still refrained. However, each time I was around it, I was wishing to smoke and a little bit jealous of Jenny and Lars for going ahead and smoking. It wasn't long before I caved and smoked with Jenny and Lars.

It felt like ages since I had smoked, and I told myself I was smart enough to not get caught. Lars' birthday happened to be the same weekend as Super Bowl Sunday, and he was graduating the upcoming

Friday in February. I was also graduating and leaving Sheppard at the end of the month, so Jenny told us she wanted us to throw a big hotel party. I couldn't think of a better idea since it was the last weekend the three of us would all be together. The three of us got together six more people, and we all pitched in on the birthday suite as well as the fifty beers we bought.

At first, everything was off to a great start, and everyone was laughing, having a great time. However, once everyone had a few beers in them, Jenny pulled Lars and I into the bathroom to ask if we wanted to get some party favors. We asked her if she meant weed, and she said of course, but what if the guy has other stuff.

So, I told Jenny to ask him since she had his number, and she told me her phone was on 5%, and she needed to use my phone so hers didn't die before he got to us. It sounded logical to me, so I gave her my phone, and with her phone in one hand and mine in the other, she asked the bartender what he could get besides weed, and she told us he had Xanax as well. Before I could say anything, Lars told her to get as many as she could.

Next thing I knew, the guy was downstairs in the hotel parking lot, and Jenny was asking me if I could go downstairs with her to make sure she was okay. This wasn't the first time she asked me, so I said of course, and into the elevator we went. While we were heading down to the lobby, she gave me her money and said, "Here you act like it's yours so he doesn't think

61

I'm setting him up by having you with me." I was drunk and took the cash.

We were in and out of the guy's car in under five minutes and back into the elevator where I gave Jenny the pills and weed. When we got back to the suite, she ran into the bathroom. Lars went banging on the door for her to open, and he saw she had some Xanax crushed on the bathroom countertop. He called me in and the three of us did a line. We went to the master bedroom away from the other guests, so they wouldn't see us rolling up the weed.

This was when the loud bangs started on our hotel door. The guests started shouting for us, and before any of us could get to the door, it came flying open, and in swarmed six OSI agents in full SWAT gear pointing M16s in our faces, yelling for us to get on the ground. Everything was happening so fast I shoved the joint into my cig pack hoping they wouldn't find it as I was on the ground.

They dragged us out into the hallway and made all nine of us get on our knees and face the wall with our hands behind our heads as they zip tied our hands. They started tossing around everything in the hotel room, and in about five minutes, they were done and had started to load us into two separate vans. The silence inside of my van was so heavy my ears started to ring.

By the time we pulled up into OSI headquarters, my buzz had completely worn off. They made us wait for the other van to show up, and then, they marched us into their holding cell and cut off the zip ties. Once we sat down, they informed us that they were splitting us up again and that the first van was going to do interrogations while the group from the second van would head out to the drug testing facility and then switch.

Of course, with my luck, I was called in first for questioning. At the time, the only thing running through my head was the question, *How could this be happening right now?* My heart sank to my stomach knowing that it hadn't even been a full year before I had found myself in serious shit once again. Two military cops escorted me from the holding cell into the interrogation room and closed the door behind themselves.

They read me my rights, and the only thing out of my mouth was that I wasn't speaking to anyone about anything until I had an attorney present. They said all right and confiscated my cell phone as evidence and then stood me up and threw me right back into the holding cell while calling out Lars' name. I should've known something was fishy when he didn't come out for half an hour, but I didn't want to believe that my best friend in the Air Force would talk to the cops.

After Lars came out, they went through questioning with the other two airmen for about an hour, and then, it was time for the drug tests. I was pretty nervous about it, because I had done a line of Xanax two and a half hours prior, so I was almost certain I was going to fail the test. They hadn't let us use the restroom this entire time, so going pee into their cup was easy. They wouldn't tell us our results when we finished but instead sent us back to our dorm rooms and told us we had a meeting with the squadron commander at 0600 sharp, which was only a couple hours away.

That next morning in the commander's office, he pulled Lars and me in at the same time and told us we were restricted to the base for thirty days, gave us the numbers to our military attorneys, and then sent us back to HQ to check in for cleaning duty, which was our new assignment until everything was sorted out.

For me, I was never going to talk, and I relayed that message to my attorney and asked her to get ready for a trial. A couple weeks later, she had me come back to her office and said to me that the prosecutors told her Jenny and Lars had spoken to OSI that night and gave statements with their attorneys that everything not only that night but everything they had heard we did since getting back from Christmas break was my idea and I had coerced them into following along with it.

I was shocked and couldn't believe what I was hearing. I asked her if she was serious and what it all meant. She informed me that it meant that OSI was following around Jenny after her party over break, and unless I had hard evidence it was all her idea, I was going down as the ringleader and would get punished harder than either Lars or Jenny, and that she needed to file a motion for discovery in order to know what the prosecution had evidence wise.

I let Jenny use my phone that night, and I never thought she'd use me to get out of trouble, so I deleted every text about anything illegal, so the only thing left on my phone were the texts she sent to the bartender herself. My attorney said a plea deal was going to be the best plan of action then. She sent me back to my HQ waiting on another call that the prosecution had handed over all of their documents. By now, it was already my nineteenth birthday, and I was depressed almost every day.

I wasn't sure how long I was going to be stuck at Sheppard, but seven weeks had passed, and the only thing I knew was that my so-called friends were fake. Sometime in April, I got a call from my attorney, and we scheduled another meeting for May to go over everything.

The entire time, I was stuck cleaning HQ, but now, I was allowed to leave the base and had picked up drinking even more than before. At that meeting, I learned that Lars and Jenny signed deals and that Jenny was getting sent back to Rhode Island with an administrative discharge and Lars was getting picked up the next day to do fifteen days in jail.

That's what they gave them for lying, meanwhile I remained in limbo, trying to fight any way I could. I never had the chance to see Jenny after that Super Bowl party, but Lars and I saw each other every single day. When he finished his fifteen days, he even came back to the same squadron and worked right beside me, knowing I knew what he had done to me. A lot of people would've gotten angry and violent, but I was trying my best to not make my circumstances any worse than they already were.

Instead, I leaned on drinking and smoking weed even more, because I didn't know how else to cope with things. Lars and I have talked since 2013 and have forgiven each other for what went down, but in the thick of it, just seeing his face made me angry. Anyway, after I calmed down in my attorney's office that afternoon in May, she let me know I had been offered a plea as well.

The United States of America was willing to offer me a bad conduct discharge instead of a dishonorable discharge if I just agreed to sign a piece of paper stating that they hadn't entrapped me in any way, shape, or form. Of course, this made me even more mad, since I knew I was set up but had no way to prove it, since nobody was being honest in their statements. I had never heard of a bad conduct discharge until then, and she informed me it was simply a misdemeanor in the eyes of the government whereas a dishonorable discharge is considered a felony.

Hearing that did bring a little ease but not much, since after that, she said they wanted me to serve six months. I asked what she thought I should do, and she said I should take the deal. When I asked why, she said because the maximum sentence I would be subject to if I didn't was twelve months in federal prison and a dishonorable discharge. That freaked me out, since the drugs we had were such a small amount.

I told her I needed time to think about it. She said I still had to go in front of the judge. The judge had to approve the plea, or they could reduce the plea sentence if they thought it was too harsh, but I wouldn't be at risk for anything more serious, so I went ahead and took the plea right then and there. She said that the next step was to get me assigned a court martial date so I could get in front of the judge. Oddly, June came and still no word of my court martial.

The Fourth of July came, and there was a huge party on base. Little did I know, but that was my last time partying in Wichita Falls, Texas. The next work day, I got a call that August 1 was my appointed date, and that we would spend the rest of the month preparing for the judge.

Things took an even weirder turn than I could've ever predicted. Two weeks before my court martial, I got pulled off cleaning duty by OSI and questioned about stolen phones. I told them they didn't have permission to go through my stuff even though I was innocent and that they'd have to wait for my attorney, but they went around it by asking my roommate if they could come in, and when they did, they magically found the stolen cell phones sitting out in the open on my bed.

They arrested me for grand larceny. I requested my phone call and let my attorney know what had happened. Wildly enough, to get camera footage to prove I never left my duty station on the days in question, it would take a judge's signature, and that coincidentally could take weeks or even months, and since we were so close to my court martial, my attorney recommended I just take an Article 15 and get on with my court martial, so I did thinking I was being smart when in reality everyone around me was pushing me toward the exit.

Hindsight is 20/20! Because I now know that if I didn't take the Article 15 they would've postponed the court martial until that was resolved. Which, they would've found me innocent. Instead, I looked guilty to the judge for not just cannabis use but for stealing as well! That in my eyes was the exact reason the judge told me I deserved a long sentence. Although, he led with that he approved the plea, so everyone could get on with their lives.

I also didn't know at the time, but the judge told me anyone discharged for drug related offenses loses their right to bear arms, so I would never again be allowed to buy a gun. Then, he hit his gavel and called for the cops to take me away. This was when they told me that I wasn't going to a military jail but instead to Wichita Falls county jail to be held.

They had me change out of my uniform and into a jumpsuit, so they could transport me. When I got there, I was clueless as to what was going on. They stripped me naked and threw powder on me and had me take a shower. After I was done, they walked me to a cell block with twenty other inmates and told me this would be my home for the next three months. I looked at them confused, and they told me that because I was a nonviolent offender that the state of Texas gave inmates two for one for good behavior, cutting my sentence in half if I didn't cause any trouble.

That little piece of information was enough to get me through my stay in county jail. Oddly enough, even though I was in jail at nineteen, because I had come from the military base, I instantly had respect from my block mates. Normally, a guy like me would've been heart checked (when your manhood gets tested) coming in and wouldn't have come out of the situation without a few bruises unless he was a punk and gave up his food, but then you got marked as prey, but they cut me slack, since I came in with my court martial docs showing United States v. Collin Gray, and they could see the court records showing I didn't snitch once.

Before I knew it, my time was up, and the same military cops that dropped me off August 1 were there with my uniform to take me back to the base to finalize my discharge by booking me a flight back to Evansville, which ended up being October 15, 2013, a week after my release from jail.

When I landed at EVV, my parents were there waiting just like they were over Christmas break. I think it's a no brainer to say we were both thrilled I was out of jail, out of the military, and back under their roof. They didn't wait very long, though, to express their concerns about my future. They wanted to know if I had any plans, and I couldn't give them a thing. You see, I literally spent my time in jail making sure I didn't focus on the outside in order to stay sane.

I was able to assure them I was going to apply for jobs, and then I would go from there. They made the comment as long as I wasn't doing what had landed me in the military in the first place that they were all right with me taking some time to figure things out.

The first employer that responded to my application was UPS, and I found myself back to work but not happy to be there. I had only been home a week or two and didn't really have much time to process what I even wanted to do with my life now that I had a fresh start again. I did get back in touch with Sparta and told him I was back home working at UPS. To say he was surprised was an understatement. He invited me over.

When I got to his house, he told me his parents had given it to him, since he and Lauren had their son. He asked how I was doing and pulled out a rolled up blunt. This was my first time smoking weed since I had went away. I told him the truth that I didn't know what I was doing with my life, but I was working until I figured it out. He immediately told me how he was selling weed and that he had somebody I should meet.

I'll never forget the first time I met Brian aka Big Poppy off Vann or Pollack. It was November 2013, and I had just gotten out of being locked up in Texas the month before and wasn't even back in Evansville two months when Sparta told me I had to meet this guy. Of course, I'm like, *What the hell? Why is this so important?* but he wouldn't tell me. He just said to show up at Amber's in an hour, so I did, and when I pulled up, I was like, *Holy shit that's a big dude*, but Sparta was always chill, so I knew he had to be a good guy.

When I got up the steps, Sparta introduced him as Big Poppy, and he quickly said Brian. I'm still not sure why I was ever there. If I was in Sparta's position with a nineteen-year-old money making machine, I wouldn't introduce him to the guy I was trying to impress so he could realize I wasn't needed, but that was really the last time I saw him until March 2014 when Sparta took off to California, and now they're both dead.

Well, I guess that's not entirely true. I saw him once or twice a month after that, but of course, it was never more than thirty minutes, and it was always at hotels with Sparta by my side. I often told Sparta we needed to hang out with Brian more to get to know each other better, but he was only focused on his hippie

71

dreams. I felt Brian had the connections to make us cannabis millionaires. Anyway, the reason I told the story was up until I got married, I often considered those days the best days of my life, and I would often get sad from time to time that it had fallen apart because of Sparta.

I looked at Brian and his wife as the perfect couple that were a great example of a true ride or die. I'm not sure why Sparta made the decision to rob both me and Brian, but I'm positive I never would've met my wife if he hadn't messed everything up.

Getting back to what was the wildest time in my life, it was March 11, 2014, right before festival season started up. Sparta and I at the time were making $1,400 a week selling cannabis, and we were starting to get cabin fever, or go stir crazy, as you might say. The old saying all work and no play makes for a real dull boy was in full effect, and we just had to escape. We caught wind of a Ratdog Show In Indianapolis. Seeing as Ratdog was created by Bob Weir, an original member of the Grateful Dead, we knew it was the perfect event to let go and blow off some stress. Like everything we did, we liked it to be a big deal, so we invited Sprout and a bunch of other buddies and took two cars up to the show. Right around the thirty-minute mark from arriving at the venue, we got some LSD out of our wallets.

Twenty-five hits to be exact, and there were five people in our car. By the time we were buying our tickets and finding our seats, the trip was starting to take off. I could always tell, because my body became as light as a cloud, and I would get a weird sensation that I might float away. The band had finished their first song *Bertha* and was starting to play *Mississippi Half-Step* when we got to our seats, which were in the dead center of the floor level aisles. However, nobody was actually sitting down. Instead, everyone was dancing around and singing along with Ratdog.

Before we knew it, the band had finished their set. The show was ending, but our trip was only halfway through, so we regrouped, and luckily, Sprout knew of an after party in the Broad Ripple neighborhood that we were all invited to.

Dead parties weren't like normal parties that you've seen in movies. Yes, the house was packed full of Deadheads, but there wasn't any alcohol in sight. Instead of everyone holding a red solo cup, there was a nitrous tank in the center of the living room, and everyone had a balloon in their hand. Of course, everyone else there was also on LSD, and in the kitchen, people weren't doing keg stands but lines of coke instead.

Upstairs, artists had filled the bedrooms with stuff for sale, which was all Grateful Dead related. We started peaking at the afterparty, and things only got weirder.

My friend China Cat Sunflower mysteriously disappeared from the party, and the rest of the group had no clue where she went. Sparta, Sprout, and I went out to the backyard to see if she was smoking, and of course, she wasn't. We did find another buddy, Josh, who was standing in the corner of the fence all by himself. When Sprout shouted, *What are you doing?* Josh sprung alive and started talking about how he was astral projecting in a different dimension.

Sparta and I busted out laughing, but we quickly calmed down as we needed to find China Cat. Luckily, our buddy, Red, was able to get her to pick up her phone, and the only thing she said was that she left with a group of people she met at the party and was on her way back. She would tell Red why, but she said she was about ten minutes away, so we decided to smoke a cig and wait. When she did get back, she shouted out the car window for us all to come over. Then, the driver popped the trunk, and we had seen the holy grail of tanks.

A whopping five foot tall, seventy pound nitrous tank. Up until this point, Sparta and I had only seen the two foot tall, twenty pound tanks. Apparently, the guy had asked China Cat if we would be interested in buying it, and knowing Sparta and me so well, she said yes on our behalf and went with them to bring it to us.

The only question was, *What do we do with it?* We couldn't fit it in Sparta's trunk, because his subs took up too much space. The next best option was to put it in the backseat and just sit on it. Now, it was getting to be two in the morning when all of this was happening, and we were faced with a tough decision.

Do we drive three hours back to Sparta's house in Newburgh, or do we go somewhere else? Turns out the night wasn't over yet, because we had another buddy from the show who lived about forty-five minutes away. That seemed like the smartest decision at the time, and I'm happy we did. When we got to our friend's house, it took two of us to carry the tank into his living room. For the next three hours until the sun came up, we just sat in a big circle laughing our faces off.

Come six in the morning, our trip had finally ended, and we were clear headed enough to make the long drive home. We decided that since we had three twenty-pound tanks in Newburgh, and the large tank was halfway empty, we would just leave it in Noblesville. When we finally got back to Sparta's house in Newburgh, the only thing anyone wanted was a fat blunt so we could call it a night even though it was ten the next morning.

Our favorite movie in high school was *Fear and Loathing in Las Vegas*. We always talked about doing a Hunter S. Thompson road trip when we got older, and after the road trip we just had, we wanted more. Something that only a guy like Hunter S. Thompson would do.

Instead of going to bed, we spent an entire afternoon masterminding how we would spend our entire summer once again hopping from state to state, festival to festival and what we were going to bring with us to make sure we had the time of our lives. We already had the cannabis accounted for, seeing as we were each selling a pound or so a day, so it was all about figuring out which party drugs we wanted to bring with us.

Our buddy, Sprout, was an OG when it came to festivals and had been connected to the scene since 1995, so it made perfect sense to reach out to Sprout and see how he could help. Boy was I glad we did, because he was the one who suggested we drive from Evansville all the way to San Francisco and to grab 10,000 hits of LSD in the form of liquid. At first, we were shocked to hear Sprout's response. We had to pick our jaws up off of the floor, but after we did that, we immediately wanted to know how much that would cost us and how we would get there and back safely.

Apparently, a liquid LSD equaling 10,000 hits only costed us $25,000 or $2.50 a hit. Like I mentioned earlier, Sparta and I were making $1,400 a week, so when we heard how cheap it was, I jumped at the chance to contribute $9,000 to the adventure! Sparta knew we needed another $16,000 just to cover the liquid and roughly another $3,000 to cover our travel expenses. Knowing we had the money to buy everything ourselves but at the same time we didn't want to spend 100% of our cash reserves, we reached out to our buddies, Bear and Milkman, to see if they wanted in on the action, since we still needed another $10,000 to hit our goal.

When they arrived at Sparta's, they had no idea why we asked them to come over. They seemed a little anxious, but after we told them every little detail, they each wanted a piece of the action. Their reactions sparked an idea in my head that if we kept doing this with each group of our friends, there was no telling how much money we could put together.

This was the first example in my life of what can be accomplished when a group of like-minded people band together and mastermind and of what real power is. Sparta and I had no idea how we were going to pull this off when we heard it, but after a week of twelve-hour long meetings with anyone who we knew in the festival scene, we rounded up to $11,000 and broke our goal!

This all happened right before my twentieth birthday, and looking back, we were insane, but I never realized it until I started talking to other people out in North Carolina and even out in California. I realized no one had the ideas and guts to do what Sparta and I did.

Sparta didn't want our day to day operations to stop, so he asked me to stay behind while he took Sprout and his girlfriend, Sky. We met up with Big Poppy to let him know he didn't have to worry about the cash flow drying up and that I was going to handle

Sparta's weight as well as my own. Big Poppy was thrilled to hear that and agreed to front me a ten pack. The very next morning, Sparta and the gang headed out first to Colorado to make a quick stop and then over to San Francisco to pick up what we were really after.

Before Sparta could even check into his hotel that first night, I had already unloaded the inventory Big Poppy gave me on credit. Big Poppy was stunned to say the least, and to my surprise, that was everything he had on him, and he asked me to wait a day so he could return with twelve more this time. When he finally made it back into town that Sunday morning, we met up for some brunch, so I could pick up my cannabis. It was just three days into Sparta's week-long road trip, and I was halfway through the second delivery. By the fifth day, I was out of product but had brought in $79,000 with $11,000 of it being profit.

When the eagle had landed back in Evansville, I rushed over to Sparta's with a Pyrex dish, some empty mouth drops containers, and some Everclear. I had no idea why other than Sprout and Sparta told me to.

Oh my gosh, I was surprised when I learned it was chemistry class. After everything and everyone got what we needed, we scattered like bugs back to each of our little cliques. For my $9,000 contribution, I received 3,600 hits and, in a month, had eaten and sold everything I had, and needless to say, had forgotten my name and ended up in the Vanderburgh County jail due to a crazy 5 vs. 4 fight in the middle of the street.

My twentieth birthday happened in this short time frame. It was one I will hardly remember and never forget at the same time. My girlfriend at the time had a best friend, and the two were inseparable. We were over at her place more than we were at the apartment we lived in. So, it only made sense that we threw a big bash at her place and invited the whole family over. Sprout brought over four fifths of Jameson, which was enough to black me out, but we will get to that in a second. Davin, Spencer, and Sparta were all there.

Up until that night, my girlfriend of four months thought I was 22 not 19 just turning 20. To my defense, we met at a bar, and I felt it wasn't smart to admit I was 19 with a fake ID. The tension was so thick, I started drinking twice as fast. Finally, more people showed up, including Sky aka the girl Sparta left his baby momma for and eventually convinced him to move away which led to him losing custody. Spencer's girlfriend was best friends with Sky, and she introduced her to the whole family and, looking back, was the very first event that started the chaos.

Anyway, now that everyone had arrived, I really let loose with the cannabis and Jameson. So hard that the last thing I remember was being in the kitchen pouring another shot. Bam! I came back to consciousness hugging the toilet on the bathroom floor.

I ran out to the living room where half of the party remained and asked what was going on. Sprout let me know that Sky had slipped a few mushroom capsules and twenty-five hits of LSD into my mouth after I stopped throwing up in the bathroom and that I snapped back because of it. That was enough to make me freak out, so I found Nikky and had her drive us back to our apartment to call it a night.

So, I thought. When we got home, she put on *Breaking Bad*. Unfortunately, my trip was starting to peak, and hearing about all of the meth and the cops was starting to send me into a spiral. I couldn't take it anymore, and there was only one thing left to do. I ran into our bedroom and unplugged the TV, picked it up, and before I could throw it out of the window, Nikky ripped it out of my arms. She sat it back down and convinced me to lay down and listen to some trance, which put me to sleep and ended the trip, thank God!

I thought this wild night would be the end of the escapades, but literally a week later in April of 2014, I had lost my girlfriend, because I wouldn't stop taking LSD, and that meant I had no place to live. The last straw was when I was staying on a friend's couch in mid-April. Again, I decided to trip and have a little get together, but these people weren't my true friends. They just wanted to see how far I'd go, and I ended up shaving off my eyebrows. The next morning, I was so embarrassed at what I had done to myself, I called Sparta up and asked him to meet me.

I had stopped my cannabis business, because I didn't have a place to keep it, and in turn, I blew through my money, because I wouldn't stop partying. Sparta said he owed me one since I kept things afloat while he was gone, and I needed it more than ever. To my surprise, Sparta was just as broke as me, and Big Poppy had cut him off. Word had spread about our summer plans, and Big Poppy didn't want to work with us anymore. I was kind of upset, and I asked if we could go inside his friend's house.

Right when I asked that, Sparta and I heard a loud scream coming from inside the home. I was unaware, but someone we both knew was trying to rob the house, and a gun was pulled. Sparta and I went running inside the home, and it was a free for all. Sparta jumped in the fight, and next thing I know, we were all out in the street. The neighbors called the cops at this point, and everyone took off running, me included. I made it six blocks before they arrested me.

This was only six months after I had been released from being locked up in Texas and sent home to await my discharge from the Air Force over cannabis. I went from broke to $20,000 in cash back to broke and in jail all in six months, and to be honest, it felt like it all happened in one day.

I was getting so high on LSD that I had convinced myself one trip I was throwing up acorns. Oddly enough, there was an ambulance across the street, and my friends had to use all of their strength to keep me from running over to the medics for help.

Looking back, I'm not surprised that I began to inject opiates later that year in June.

I remember the day vividly, the day I shot up heroin for the first time. It was with a girl who graduated from my high school a few years ahead of me. I had run into her at a local gas station, and we started talking about old times. She asked if I wanted to hang out and catch up, and I thought, *Why not?*

We went to her friend's apartment, and as soon as we walked in, I could smell the pungent aroma of burnt rubber. I knew what was going on, but I didn't say anything. She showed me how to prepare the heroin in a spoon, and as she finished, she tied a rubber band-like thing around my arm and stuck the needle in. I felt the rush almost immediately, and I was flying high. It was the most intense sensation I had ever felt.

But then, she took the rubber band off, and I felt like I was going to die. The rush was too intense, and my body couldn't handle it. I started throwing up, and I couldn't stop for two hours. It was the worst experience of my life, and I swore I would never do it again, however, my body was already hooked!

The most shocking part of that day was when her four-year-old daughter walked in on her mom and me. She didn't seem to notice what was going on, but her mom quickly told her that we were just taking our medicine. The little girl started walking around, pointing at her arm, saying she wanted to take her medicine, too.

It was heartbreaking to see how drugs and addiction could affect an innocent child's life.

From that day on, my life became centered around shooting up. I was consumed by the need to use, and everything else in my life took a backseat. The high became my escape from reality, but it came at a great cost. My health deteriorated, my relationships fell apart, and I lost everything I had ever loved.

In November 2014, I received a phone call from my close friend Aaron Brown, who revealed to me that he had tested positive for hepatitis C. I was shocked and scared, because I had been stupid enough to share needles with him in the past. I decided to get tested for the virus, and a few days later, my fears were confirmed: I had hepatitis C, too.

My entire life, I felt invincible, believing that nothing could bring me down. However, receiving the news that I had hepatitis C shattered that illusion. I realized that I was just as vulnerable as anyone else, and that I needed to take my health seriously.

I went to see a liver specialist who explained my treatment options. He recommended the newest medication, which had a high cure rate, but was out of this world expensive. I was anxious and uncertain about how my parents would react to the news. My next thought was *How would I afford the treatment?* Fortunately, I still had my military insurance which covered the entire $80,000 and the support of my parents, who helped me get to the hospital every week for my tests.

The treatment was intense and came with severe side effects, including fatigue, headaches, and nausea. I felt like I was living in a fever dream, and it was difficult to complete everyday tasks. However, there was no way my family was going to let me stop my treatment.

Looking back throughout the treatment, I wish I prayed constantly, asking God to give me the strength to endure. I had the support of my loved ones, who provided comfort and encouragement when I needed it most. Their presence in my life was a reminder that I was not alone in my struggles, but I can only imagine how much easier it would've been if I had God and a congregation to lean on as well.

The 12-week treatment felt like an eternity, but I refused to give up hope. I believed that I would be cured, and I kept my focus on that goal. In July 2015, I received the good news that I had been waiting for: my doctor declared that I was cured of hepatitis C. Not only that, but my liver had fully healed and returned to normal function.

The sense of relief and joy that I felt was indescribable. I had been given a second chance at life, and I felt extremely lucky, but it still wasn't enough to end my obsession with shooting up.

This experience taught me the importance of taking care of my physical and emotional health. I realized that I needed to make conscious choices to nourish my body and soul, such as eating a balanced diet, exercising, and seeking emotional support when needed.

Thinking back to this difficult time in my life, I see how God was with me every step of the way. Keeping my insurance active during my entire treatment when I had been out of the Air Force for a year at this point was only one of the many ways. The fact that Aaron had the courage and respect to call me so I could get help, and I believe that's another instance of his presence. He gave me the strength to endure the treatment and the courage to face my fears and admit to my parents what was going on so I could get help. He surrounded me with people who loved and cared for me, and who provided the support and encouragement that I needed instead of turning their backs on me.

Today, as crazy as it sounds, I'm grateful for this experience, as it has taught me important lessons about life, faith, and perseverance. I know that I will face challenges in the future, but they will be nothing in comparison to the challenges I've already gone through.

In the depths of despair, my life took a harrowing turn, leading me down a treacherous path that eventually led to the cold, unforgiving streets of homelessness. The haunting echoes of my past reverberated through the shattered remnants of my soul, each step a painful reminder of the choices that had brought me here.

One of the struggles during my treatment was an incident in February 2015 where I was pulled over in my car and I didn't have any car insurance that became a poignant turning point, a stark reminder of the consequences borne from my battle with addiction. As the weight of my actions bore down upon me, I found myself stripped of a fundamental piece of identification: my driver's license. It served as a tangible reminder of the paths I had strayed from, a physical manifestation of the barriers I faced on the road to recovery.

In the absence of my driver's license, life took on a surreal quality. Simple tasks became arduous challenges, as each interaction required alternative means of identification. The freedom once associated with the open road was replaced by a sense of confinement, a reminder that my actions had consequences that extended far beyond my immediate struggles.

Yet, even in the darkest moments, a flicker of hope burned within my soul. It was as if a divine presence lingered in the background, patiently waiting for me to find the strength to confront my demons and embark on the path of redemption. The return of my driver's license became an emblem of hope, a beacon guiding me toward a future filled with purpose, sobriety, and the unwavering belief that no matter how far we stray, God's love is ever-present, ready to extend a hand and guide us back to the path of restoration.

The straw that broke the camel's back! Sometime before the springtime of 2016. My father's wedding ring had once symbolized a bond of love and commitment, a cherished heirloom meant to be passed down through generations. However, in the grips of addiction, desperation clouded my judgment, and I made a fateful decision that shattered the delicate threads connecting me to my family's history. I traded the symbol of eternal love for a temporary escape, selling it to fuel my insatiable craving for heroin.

When my parents found out what I had done they told me I was no longer welcomed under their roof. With trembling hands and a heavy heart, I sought solace in the dark alleys, isolated from the warmth and security that once embraced me. The venomous grip of withdrawal tightened its hold, demanding its tribute of agony. Each day became a relentless battle, not against the world, but against the demons that resided within.

As the relentless claws of addiction gnawed at my sanity, the bitter reality of my circumstances began to take hold. Shelter became an abandoned doorway, providing a meager respite from the unforgiving elements. Hunger gnawed at my stomach, a constant companion in my destitution. The world, bustling with life and purpose, seemed to pass me by, an invisible specter haunting the peripheral vision of society.

Yet, even in the darkest corners of despair, a flicker of hope dared to burn within my heart. For it was in the depths of my homelessness that I confronted the harsh realities of my addiction, stripped bare of the illusions that had once clouded my vision. It was a crucible, forging resilience and a fervent desire for redemption.

Through the countless nights spent beneath the starless sky, I began to piece together fragments of shattered dreams. The pain and isolation that once defined my existence became the catalyst for change, a searing flame that burned away the veils of denial. Each painful step forward carried the weight of remorse, but also the potential for healing and renewal.

In the eyes of those who passed by, I saw reflections of judgment and pity. But within the depths of my being, I knew that I was more than my circumstances. The journey of redemption had begun, guided by the unwavering belief that I could reclaim my identity and rebuild the broken fragments of my life.

With the support of compassionate souls who recognized my struggle, I found solace in the embrace of recovery programs and the unwavering love of those who refused to abandon me to the clutches of addiction. Each day of sobriety became a testament to the strength that lay dormant within me, a beacon of resilience that illuminated the path forward.

I emerged from the darkness, a survivor of the shadows, scarred but not defeated. The path of homelessness became a stepping stone toward a life reclaimed, a reminder of the depths from which I had risen. Though the road to healing was arduous and fraught with challenges, it became a testament to the enduring power of hope and the indomitable human spirit.

The journey from homelessness to restoration which you will read more about in the rest of my memoir, taught me that redemption is not confined to the realm of fairy tales but is a tangible reality, awaiting those who dare to confront their past and embrace the possibility of transformation. As I walked away from the desolate streets that once held me captive, I carried with me a newfound understanding—that even amidst the wreckage of my choices, a brighter future awaited, illuminated by the flame of redemption and the unwavering grace of second chances.

In spring 2016, I was tricked into going to a hotel room and was robbed. I had been shooting up for two years at this point and was contacted by James, and he asked if I could come over to his hotel room, because he had some money he owed me but no ride to bring it to me. I said sure and got a ride to take me over to the hotel. When I hopped out of the car and headed toward the hotel door, I got a weird feeling.

When I went inside, it was just him sitting on the bed with a needle in his hand. He told me to lock the door and help him find his vein. As soon as I locked the door, his closet door came flying open, and two dudes came running out, and one of them even had a baseball bat. I tried to turn around and run out, but they grabbed me before I could get the door unlocked. The three of them surrounded me, shouting and yelling to give them some painkillers.

Apparently, I had the only source of painkillers in the tri-state. At least, until the first of the month came around, and everyone got their monthly refill. I could tell these guys were detoxing hard and thought I'd have something on me. I didn't even have spare change on me let alone pills. When they realized I wasn't dumb enough to walk around with pockets full of goodies, they rushed out the hotel room, leaving me behind. My shirt was all torn, but everything else was normal. I got up, left the room, and went back to my friend's house who I had been staying with.

I called my mom begging for her help once again, and the only words she could gather were the words for how I needed to go straight to rehab. I agreed to go to the detox center for the third time but only after I went and got high. After I was ready to go to the center, my mom picked me up, and off we went. When we got there, the intake center was packed. We had to wait roughly thirty minutes before we could be seen and checked in.

I didn't realize it, but the Xanax I took while I shot up the heroin before my mom picked me up was really starting to kick in. When the nurse took us back to get vitals and to fill out the paperwork, I started to fall asleep. The nurse didn't notice at first, but after about five minutes of talking to me with my eyes closed, the nurse forced my mom to take me to the ER for fear I was overdosing. My mom freaked out once again, and off to the ER we went.

The doctors rushed me to a private room immediately, and I became enraged. Here, I was enjoying my "last" high, and here they were, all panicked and shouting, threatening to inject me with Narcan. I just lost it on everyone, my mom included, to the point that the hospital security came to the room and threatened to force me to calm down. All that did was piss me off even more, so I got in his face and scared him to the point he left the room, and they decided my mom was the only one who could calm me down. After about twenty minutes of just me and my mom in the room, I was calm, and the doctors came back in and determined I wasn't overdosing, which I already knew.

So, back to the detox center we went, where I was checked in, and then, I slept for thirty-six hours straight. When I woke up, I escaped the facility by running out of the cafeteria doors, because they were the only doors unlocked. Since then, they've added additional security measures to ensure I was the last person to escape. I was officially on the run about ten miles outside of town with no phone, so I ran until I saw a synagogue. When I got inside, all sweaty and in sweats, I was greeted by a nice Indian woman. She asked if I needed help, and I replied I need to use a phone if she had one. She gave me their phone, and just like that, my ride was on the way. Before I knew it, I was in another trap house, getting a shot ready for my veins.

This entire time I've had an arrest warrant out for me and actually had one for a few months at this point. The sheriff's department was looking for me, but I wasn't going to let them stop me from shooting up. At this point in my life, I was convinced I was doomed to a lifetime of needles and spoons, and I just wanted to be left alone. In my head, I had blown my shot at an amazing wealthy life, and all I wanted to do was get high and forget my failure. Little did I realize at that time was, every day we wake up is our chance to do better and make life a success. About a couple weeks after my escape and from hopping from couch to couch, I broke down and asked my mom to get me out of Evansville.

Seeking God Set Me Free

I didn't want to go back to the detox center right next to town. I wanted to be hours away in hopes I wouldn't get arrested and thrown back in jail, which at this point happened once every four to six months, and I was in a courthouse about one or two times a month.

My time at Teen Challenge, the faith-based treatment center, was definitely one of the most important times in my life. I went there June 24, 2016 to June 24, 2017, and if there was ever a time I couldn't screw up, this was it. My mom had arranged to pick me up from Ksand's house. Ksand, rest her soul, let me spend the night, since I was on the run from the cops. Teen Challenge was a two-hour drive north of Evansville in Terre Haute, so my mom picked me up bright and early. Needless to say, the withdrawals were in full effect. When we were about ten minutes from the center, I asked for her to pull over, so I could use the restroom.

I went inside the CVS we pulled into, and in the bathroom, I pulled out a syringe I made the night before and stuck it right into my arm. Feeling much better, I ran out the store to hop back in the van. The Teen Challenge center was definitely not what I expected. I imagined a Passages Malibu, and what I walked into turned out to be Bible Bootcamp. Teen

Challenge is an international Pentecostal faith-based rehabilitation organization.

We weren't allowed to have access to our cell phones, computers, newspapers, TV, or anything that wasn't Christian related. We were allowed mp3 players but only with Christian music. We went to church for three hours on Sundays, Wednesdays, and Thursdays. On Mondays, Tuesdays, and Fridays, we had bible study classes from 1-5 p.m., and Saturdays were our days off. Teen Challenge was a twelve-month long program.

When my mom and I arrived that first day, I had no clue if I would be able to stay the entire year, but I knew I'd be in prison if I didn't try. The intake coordinator reached out to the courthouse, and my arrest warrants were suspended as long as I was at the treatment center. Over the course of the year, when we weren't at church or studying our bibles, we were doing manual labor for the members of the various churches we visited in Terre Haute. We did everything from cleaning the churches, landscaping, construction work, and moving services.

Intake day is always the most awkward day in anyone's journey to their best self. Everyone knows you're high, and you know everyone is mad, because they wish they were, but the second day is always the most painful day. That's because you have nothing to use, and the hard reality comes crashing down that you have hit rock bottom. This is the day withdrawals are at their worst, and all I wanted to do, all anyone wants to do is run away and get high.

I'm so thankful for my mentors and pastors, because they didn't let me cave. Instead, they asked if they could pray for me. Now, I'd be lying if I said I wanted to be prayed for, but I said yes, because I figured I could finally get them to shut up and allow me to leave the center. This day and this moment specifically will forever be burned into my memory.

When the men surrounded me and started praying in tongues, which if you aren't familiar with the gift of tongues, review the book of Acts in the bible, I thought to myself that my mom had dropped me off at a cult. I had watched a few History channel episodes on Pentecostals, and I peeked my eye open to make sure there wasn't a person about to throw a snake on me. Once I felt comfortable, I closed my eyes, and I let their prayers cover me like a warm blanket. I began to pray, because one of the men had asked God to end my withdrawals, and that was something I could get behind. I started to feel a hot sensation engulf me like flames.

I started to become sweaty, and next thing I knew, my symptoms of withdrawal were gone. I was so shocked and at a loss for words. In the moment, I decided to stay at the center for a month and go from there. To be honest, the only thing I can remember from that first month is going to the local park to play a game of basketball. The upcoming eleven months were certainly a pivotal moment in my life, and I had absolutely no clue the transformation I was about to go through.

My mindset was to treat it like any of my previous stays in jail, but God had a different plan. My first visit came at the four-month mark. After being there an entire month and having gotten to know the men I was living with, I decided to make it to my first visit and to go from there.

In late August, two months into my journey, our church Cross Tabernacle was holding a baptizing service, and for some reason, I had an irresistible urge to sign up. When I try to think about why I decided to get baptized and announce my faith to the world, the only thing I can come up with is that my gut told me I'd regret not signing up, and I can confirm to this day I've never regretted doing it. Following my gut was the right decision!

Up to this point in my life, I always felt an awkward sensation when I was in church or when I was just simply talking about God. As a child, church was just something my mom forced me to go to on Sundays. I would always admit I believed in God, but my only reason was because I thought I was supposed to, and now in Teen Challenge, I had felt God's love and mercy when he completely removed my withdrawals on that second morning.

I have gone through opiate withdrawals at least a hundred times in the 730 days I stuck a needle in my arm and had tried to quit just as many times, so for me, this was enough to show me God is real. After that moment, it became a whole lot easier to imagine staying in the program for the remaining ten months.

Another big component in the program is going around to churches to share our testimonies in hopes that there was at least one person in the pews that was getting hope that everything would be all right. No matter what your pain or struggle was, God would take the burden away from you. This was only for students who had made it to the four-month mark, and that they could tell had the desire to share.

We had to put together a short five-minute speech about our times in addiction and the nightmares we had created with our lives. Then, after two minutes, we switched to speak about the works God was doing in our lives. This was all to give glory to God for setting us free and to hopefully prevent others from making the same mistakes.

Going from church to church to share my story began to be therapeutic for me. Giving my testimony mixed with our rigorous weekly schedules made time fly. The first six months had passed, and I could say I was halfway through! I finally saw the light at the end of the tunnel. But then, it hit me that I would need to start figuring out a plan for my life outside of Teen Challenge. Pressure instantly came into the picture. I knew this feeling; it was the exact feeling I got when I became a junior at Castle High School, and everyone started asking me what I was going to do after graduation.

Quickly, I turned to prayer, because I was taught that when we pray nonstop, God gives us the answers to our questions. I was trying my best to break the cycle of my past, and I knew that I needed to lean into God if I wanted to be successful. Lucky for me, I had another six months before being sent out into the cold world and used that time in Teen Challenge to figure out that I wanted to go into missions.

As far as our day-to-day routine went, there wasn't any change to it until graduation. Wake up, eat breakfast, morning devotions, leave to work, back for lunch, bible study, dinner, free time, nightly devotions, sleep. The only thing left to motivate us was the scheduled weekends we got to leave the center and be with our families.

To be completely honest, I'd be lying if I said I had this book in my brain when I was going through the program. However, I did have a vision of me leaving my hometown and working in God's will. If you had asked me in the program if I thought I'd be married within four years and that I would be a realtor selling millions of dollars' worth of real estate within three years, I would've called you crazy. I will admit I still had doubts in my mind that my past was going to hold me back from my dreams. I vividly remember the question,

God are you going to make this attempt at sobriety different than all the attempts I screwed up? I will never forget the day I received my real estate license and realized that God had heard all of my prayers and answered them.

Back to the story, I spent a lot of time daydreaming in the last six months of Teen Challenge and praying nonstop that if He just gave me a calling, not a career but a calling, there would be no way I would ever be tempted to relapse. However, none of those thoughts were half as cool as the life God has actually blessed me with. I got to a point where I quit making things up to do outside of Teen Challenge and said, "God, whatever happens, happens," and in doing that, I surrendered my own desires, so His could shine through.

I loved going to church events outside of church in the remaining months at the center, because it was the only time outside of our designated family visits that we got to socialize. As summer was approaching, everyone needed our help. In the last month of Teen Challenge, I found out I had completed over 800 hours of community service and had spent over 2,000 hours studying every word God had ordained to be in the bible. Teen Challenge wasn't successful for everyone.

Josh Burgess was a shining light in my journey through rehab. From day one, he exuded an energy and positivity that inspired us all. Despite his own battles with heroin addiction, he always had a kind word and a helping hand for the newcomers.

I remember one Fourth of July, his family threw a pool party for the center. It was a day filled with laughter and joy, a much-needed respite from the daily struggles of rehab. Josh was in his element, welcoming everyone with open arms and ensuring that everyone had a good time.

But despite his seemingly unbreakable spirit, Josh succumbed to his temptations during one of our trips home. He left the program for another center in his hometown, where he was later found dead from an overdose.

Josh's passing was a devastating blow to all of us. It was a stark reminder that addiction is something that can strike anyone, no matter how strong they appear on the outside. But it also taught me a valuable lesson: we cannot hide our struggles from one another. We must lean on each other for strength in our times of weakness, for it is only through vulnerability and connection that we can truly heal.

In many ways, Josh's spirit lives on in all of us who were fortunate enough to cross paths with him. His kindness, generosity, and resilience continue to inspire us to this day, a reminder that even in our darkest moments, there is hope and the possibility for redemption.

The pain of loss is a heavy burden to bear, and it's something that I had to grapple with all too often during my time at Teen Challenge. Josh Burgess wasn't the only one I met there who succumbed to addiction. Stevie Lockman was another beautiful soul gone too soon from an overdose.

Stevie had already gone through the program a couple of years before I arrived that summer. His return surprised everyone, as we thought he was doing so well. Stevie came from a long line of pastors, and I recognized the pressure he was feeling to follow in their footsteps. He didn't spend the full year in the program, and he misled everyone into thinking he was healed.

When I graduated from the program in July 2017, Stevie invited me to speak at one of his addiction treatment services. It was an honor to be asked, and I quickly jumped at the opportunity. But little did I know that this would be the last time I ever saw him.

The pain of losing someone you care about is never easy to bear. But Stevie's passing taught me that life is fragile and fleeting, and that we must cherish every moment we have with those we love. No matter how strong the feeling is to hide our struggles, we can't deny our loved ones the chance to help us and support us in our journey toward healing.

Although Stevie's life was cut tragically short, his memory lives on in the hearts and minds of those his path had crossed. His kindness, compassion, and unwavering faith continue to inspire me to this day, reminding me that even in the face of adversity, there is hope for a brighter tomorrow.

Even though all of this craziness was going on, I had to stay focused. I leaned into my faith even more, and I spent a ton of time thinking about what I was going to do with the rest of my life after Teen Challenge. At the age of 23, I wasn't able to tell my family I had figured anything out. I'm sure they were thinking, not this again. This led me to become nervous once again about leaving the center, and when I was at a church revival, we had a special music group visit, and I was introduced to a three-year faith-based program in Charlotte, North Carolina.

As it was the only thing I had heard that would allow me to do missions as well as leave Evansville, I jumped on the chance. To me, the Fire School of Ministry was an opportunity to leave behind a town that reminded me of nothing but pain and to explore God's world. I had a lot of guilt asking my parents for help fresh out of rehab, because I had taken so much from them over the years due to my addiction. I felt a little better about it when I asked and they jumped at the chance to help. I had been sober for a year in August 2017, but I had no clue the real challenges had yet to come.

Not out of the Woods Yet

If you thought this was the end of the story, and God had made it all rainbows and sprinkles from the point I graduated on, you'd be extremely mistaken. You see, I was only 22-23 in rehab, and even though with God's help I was able to conquer my horrible addiction to anything that got me high, I was still a newborn baby in the faith, and the wolves were certainly waiting for me.

When I got to Charlotte, I had a heavy rock of anxiety and nerves in my stomach. I had absolutely no idea why I was there other than I couldn't stay in Evansville, and missions was the word I kept hearing over and over in my head. In the two months I was there, I managed to break numerous rules and found myself kicked out of the program that fall in October 2017.

I felt ashamed to have to make the phone call home to my parents to tell them once again their son had screwed up a good opportunity. At this moment, the only thing on my mind was how I needed to get a job to create income, so I didn't have to go crawling back to Evansville. I would've rather left this earth than go back, so I did something I had never done before when faced with failure and hard challenges! I screamed out to God, begging in his son's name to fix what I had once again ruined.

Nervous of going broke, I found myself applying to every restaurant in town and got hired to do a job bartending at a fine dining establishment. I had worked in restaurants before, so the atmosphere was something I was comfortable with.

Like high school, I made it a point to befriend everyone in the restaurant. If I was going to survive and thrive, I couldn't risk going unnoticed, and before I knew it, I was back out at the bars three nights a week. Halloween had come and gone, and it was that weird in between time of Halloween and Thanksgiving when I heard about DJ Tiesto coming to Charlotte.

I felt excited to buy the tickets, and I found a group of coworkers to join. Up to this point, even though I was going to bars and clubs, I was sticking to a one drink maximum. That night, going to see Tiesto was the first time I blacked out drinking since my days in the Air Force.

I remember looking at my cell phone around midnight before everything went black, and I came to on the ground of a gas station. When I came to, I was in a state of panic, and the only thing I could think to do was to run to my car and to hurry back to my place. The only catch was that the silver Nissan Altima I saw sitting next to the gas pump wasn't my silver Nissan Altima.

You see, when I hopped in the driver's side, there was a passenger in the car. I looked at them and asked why they were in my car, and they started screaming at me. They pulled out a gun and said they would shoot me if I didn't get out of the car, so I flung the car door open and bolted down the parking lot.

While I was running away, I saw another silver Nissan that I just knew was my car. So, I ran over and tried opening up the driver's side door, and it was locked. I was so panicked with what had just happened that I started elbowing the glass window in hopes I could shatter it and get into my car that I thought I had locked the keys inside in my blacked-out state.

While I was trying to get inside the other Nissan Altima, I heard a siren and turned around to see a Charlotte Police car pulling up. Thinking to myself I really screwed up this time, I stopped trying to break into the car to talk to the cops. Next thing I knew, I was in the back of the cop car while they went to interview the gas station clerk.

I started to fill with grief and remorse for what had happened, and I became very nauseous. So nauseous to the point I had to start banging on the cop car's windows to get the other officers' attention. When he flung the door open to scream, I leaned over and puked all over his shoes.

What happened next was an intervention from God! The cop asked me what was wrong with me, and I went from actually vomiting to having word vomit with the cop. I told him I had just gotten out of a year-long rehab and was out at a club drinking for the first time. He asked me if I thought it was a smart decision, and when I told him it was beyond stupid, he asked me if I was okay with going to the hospital. He said if I could go to the hospital then they wouldn't arrest me or write me up for anything, so I said how long until the ambulance can get here. About an hour later, I found myself back in an ER.

The doctors held me in a room for an hour or so while they monitored my condition. I ended up being released and had to take a taxi back to my place. When I got home, I realized I still needed to find my car, so I called the group I was with the previous night, and they informed me that I had actually left it in the parking lot of the nightclub, which meant that neither of the two silver Nissan Altimas at the gas station were mine. I ordered an Uber to take me back to the club, and when I got there, my keys were on the driver's side floor, and the doors were unlocked.

To this day, nobody, including me, knows how I made it from the club, which closed at 3 a.m., to the gas station where I regained consciousness at 6 a.m., but I do know God kept me safe that day. As wild of a night/day as that was, I went in to work a shift less than twelve hours after that like nothing had ever happened.

Before I knew it, Christmas time was here, and I was off to visit my family in the Midwest. It had been six months since I graduated, and my parents were excited to hear how things were going. I didn't have much of any news besides the fact that I was bartending.

While I was visiting my family, I received a message from an old friend on Facebook. I cautiously responded, and to my surprise, he had moved out to northern California. I used to get cannabis from him when Brian was out of stock before I became addicted to opiates. Sparta had briefly introduced us in the winter of 2013-2014, and he was trying to build another business like the one we had.

I can't believe at the time of writing this book, it's been nine almost ten years that Sparta and I were the biggest advocates for cannabis in Evansville, making sure that the meth addicts and opiate addicts could use the cannabis to break free from those horrible drugs if they truly wanted to, but it's certainly a reminder of how fast time flies when you're recreating your life.

Anyway, I had to turn the old colleague down on his offer. You see, moving cannabis across the country from state to state even if it's a legal state to another legal state has a high probability of ending in you getting caught by the feds and then spending, oh, I don't know, say the next ten years of your life in prison.

Now, just because I decided to turn him down on his offer doesn't mean I didn't have any ideas of my own. Ever since I was sixteen, I had wanted to move to California to legally grow cannabis. I had this vision of creating a strain that would be such an amazing smoke that people would instantly stop using drugs that were physically addicting and that they could then turn their lives around. So, I pitched him the idea, and he loved it. He loved it so much that he agreed to let me live with him once I saved up enough to move.

I finally had a sense of direction and a great excitement that I would be accomplishing a childhood dream. After our conversation, my family and I spent the week together celebrating Christmas. This was the first Christmas in years that everyone could come together and celebrate and not feel like there was a large elephant in the room that everyone was ignoring.

Visiting with my grandparents that winter was very special as it was the second to last time we got to visit before their passing. Looking back on life, I realized something pretty simple. We as humans look at life in the timeframe of years, but we should really be looking at our personal relationships in a different numerical sense. For example, if you visit your parents twice a year and they have five years left on this planet, you would say, *Oh, I have five years left with my parents*, but in reality, you only have ten more visits before you can never spend time with your parents again.

I spent a week with my family before I had to return to Charlotte, and I still say it wasn't long enough. When I got back, however, life was waiting, and so was everyone else who had nothing better to do than party.

When I landed in Charlotte, a friend of mine who was a cocktail waitress at a strip club invited me out for their New Year's Eve celebration, and I wasn't one to turn down a good time. I got to the club, and it felt like everyone was waiting for me to get there. They probably were waiting, since I had a reputation of always having the best cannabis around. However, they were already drinking, and when I showed up, they expected me to play catch up. My friend had brought me a shot of tequila and a Jameson Dr. Pepper. After finishing my drinks, I whipped out a blunt and asked everyone "Who wants to smoke?"

My friend and three of her friends raised their hands, and we hurried into the back room. They couldn't be back there too long, so we smoked the blunt as fast as we could so they could get back on the floor doing what they do best. The club closed around 3 a.m., so when that happened, we all left, but not without smoking the other two blunts I had. I was pretty faded, but I was still confident I could make the thirty-minute drive back to my house.

About halfway home, my eyes became very heavy, so I rolled my windows down and turned my music all the way up to prevent me from falling asleep behind the wheel. Unfortunately, that wasn't good enough, because the next thing I knew, everything went black. It felt like just a second had passed, but next thing I knew, I had crashed my car into the ditch going close to 60 in a 45. According to records, I drove through someone's yard before hitting a culvert. The collision broke my Altima's front axle. The crash was so intense that the flooring of my car was completely ripped out and when I looked down, I saw the grass below where the gas and brake pedals were supposed to be.

I became extremely panicked, and I checked my limbs to make sure nothing was missing or broken. I realized I was okay, so I went to grab my phone to see if I could call for help, and the screen was completely shattered. I looked around for a clue as to where I had crashed, and the street sign I saw told me I was about seven miles away from my house. I hopped out of the car and immediately fell to the ground. Something had happened to my ankle, and I wasn't able to support my weight on it.

Determined to get back to my house, I took off jogging/limping. The entire way home, I was praying to God, asking him to make everything better. I was apologizing for my weakness and for slipping back to my old ways. By the time I made it home, the sun had come up, and I knew somebody would see my crashed car sitting in the ditch.

I didn't find out that God had been protecting me until the cops showed up on my doorstep. They wanted to know what happened, and after I told them, they cited me with leaving the scene of an accident. What the cop said next is what made me realize I had God's hand on me during this traumatic experience. He said that they found my student ID to my Christian college in the debris and that they were glad to see I wasn't seriously injured. In this moment, I knew God had blinded them from pursuing the possibility that I had been under the influence of something. In the past, when stuff like this happened, I thought I was lucky or had outsmarted the other people.

After the tow truck dropped off my wrecked car and the cops had left my house, I decided it was time to call my folks and fill them in on what had just happened less than twenty-four hours after returning home. They were in shock to hear what happened, but they were ultimately relieved to hear that I was okay.

To this day, I walk with a slight limp and am reminded of the accident every day. I ended 2017 with a little bang and no idea of what to do next. Thankfully, my parents found a new vehicle for me and made the trip out east to deliver it. When they headed back to Indiana, I made a vow to leave North Carolina before the end of 2018 like my buddy and I talked about. God had once again reminded me of how precious the gift of life is and how we should never take a single day on Earth for granted.

It took me a few months to save up $600, but in June 2018, I booked my one-way ticket from Charlotte to Sacramento. Most of you reading this probably paused and are thinking to yourselves, *Wow, this guy moved across the entire United States with only $600*, and I promise you, that's not an exaggeration.

When I landed in the capitol of California, I had this sense of calmness sweep over me like I had finally gotten to the place I was meant to be. My buddy that I spoke with during my Christmas visit scooped me up and took me back to his place. With no money, no car, and only my suitcase full of clothes, I decided I would build a new life from the ground up. One, I could be proud of. A new life that would make God smile!

Trying to Live a Christlike Life

It was June 18, 2018 when I landed in Sacramento. I had no idea of what I was going to do other than help my friend grow medical cannabis. For the last eight years of my life, I had only been a liaison connecting people with the product. I was nervous about making the transition from broker to grower, but what felt like my entire life had been leading up to this point, and I wasn't about to screw it up.

That summer was one of the most difficult summers of my life. I met my wife that summer, a true Godsend. She was honestly the only thing that got me through it. I realized very quickly that I went from expert smoker to ignorant farmer.

I decided to take a step back from growing and move back into the broker role, and I hit the road. I felt most comfortable there, and I enjoyed talking to medical dispensary owners all over California about how our medicine would revolutionize and eliminate the country's drug problems.

After two months, I saved up enough cash to rent an apartment and buy a car. My wife and I had only known each other for a few weeks at this time, so believe me when I tell you God is why we are together. I literally had no furniture, only a twin size air mattress, and she spent the night, anyway.

My wife comes from a family of entrepreneurs, mainly real estate, so she was accustomed to the finer things in life, which is why my only reasonable explanation for her not breaking up with me is that our marriage had been ordained by God long before we were a thought in our mothers' heads.

The $5,000 I had saved up over the two months I was living with my friend was back to $0, and I had the biggest smile on my face. It was so weird, because $5,000 was the largest chunk of money I had spent in a longtime. I was now broke once again, but I knew this time it wasn't from partying but from investing in my future, so I praised God and thanked Him.

You might think it's weird that someone who spent $5,000 to acquire a $1,800 a month rental expense as well as expenses from owning a car and is now broke wasn't stressed but truly happy, and I promise you, it was because I knew God was standing right next to me, and now that I had my soulmate next to me, I felt invincible.

At this point in my life, I had made it a habit to talk to God every day. I was thanking Him for this new life, but little did I know, this life wasn't my purpose, and God had made a promise to me He planned to keep. You see, when before I was even a teenager, one day, watching TV, I saw a show come on, and it was about these New York City realtors and these million-dollar homes they were selling. I was so amazed by this show, I said to myself, now this is what I want to be when I grow up.

Thinking back to when my engagement took place in June 2019, I am filled with awe and gratitude for how God was with me every step of the way, guiding me toward the perfect moment to pop the question. The six weeks leading up to the proposal were a flurry of activity, as I carefully planned every detail with God's loving guidance and direction.

It all started with finding the perfect engagement ring. With each prayerful step, I sought God's wisdom and discernment in selecting the ring that would best represent the depth of my love for her. Finally, after weeks of searching, I found the perfect ring that spoke to my heart and soul, and I knew without a doubt that this was the one.

But I didn't want the proposal itself to be anything short of perfect either. So, with the help of her close friend, Becca, we planned a surprise proposal at the Oracle Baseball Stadium in San Francisco. Every aspect of the proposal was carefully planned to create a memorable and unforgettable experience for her.

As I nervously waited for the day to arrive, I prayed for God's peace and calm to descend upon me. I knew that I wanted to ask her to be my partner in life in a way that would touch her heart and leave an indelible impression on her mind. With each passing day, my anticipation grew, and I longed for the moment when I could finally ask her to marry me.

Finally, the day arrived, and we hit the road for our three hour drive that was ahead of us. After meeting up with Becca and her boyfriend Thomas we took a cab to the park. As I looked at her, I knew that I had found my forever. With Becca videotaping by my side, I asked her what was on the jumbotron. When she looked up she saw her name and that I was asking her to marry me. When she turned back to look at me I was on one knee with the ring in my hand and as she said "yes" with tears streaming down her face, I knew that God had been there all along, watching over us and guiding us toward this moment.

Looking back, I am overwhelmed with gratitude for how God orchestrated every detail of our engagement, from finding the perfect ring to planning the perfect proposal. As we embarked on this journey together, I knew that God was going to continue to be our guide and our rock, watching over us and guiding us through life's ups and downs, always with His loving care and grace.

We returned back home and began talking about the future, our visions for it, and our beliefs, and she made it clear to me she didn't want to marry someone who didn't have a career. At that moment, I had to decide which I loved more, cannabis or my fiancée.

I decided to think about other paths I could take, and this was when she brought up becoming a realtor. That led me to visualize it, which brought back a childhood memory racing back to the forefront of my mind. I had always hoped, and I still do hope, that there will be a day in my lifetime where cannabis would be off the controlled substance list and accepted nationwide as a medicine, but I thought to myself, until that day comes, I'm going to sell the most expensive thing that people will buy.

I was very nervous about my past prohibiting me from being able to obtain a license to sell. I had a mindset, however, that I would never make a decision based on the unknown, or as I say fear. So, I did what I do best, and that's tell God if you've brought this into my life, then please make everything work out. I know the prayer isn't pretty, but it shows you one very important thing. It shows you that there are things in this world we can and will never be able to control, so we should leave that to the big man upstairs.

Relinquishing the uncontrollable to Him releases so much stress from our minds, and that everything that is meant to be will be no matter what obstacle gets in your way and no matter what self-doubting thought is going on in your head at the present moment in time.

I found a real estate school, and I signed up for classes the very next morning after our deep conversation. The instructor told me that an average realtor pays roughly $3,000 from the start of classes to when you are a part of the MLS. It was certainly a thought in my head that I could spend a boatload of money just to be denied, but then, a second thought came in right after that. The thought was a very weird one and kind of had me questioning why I was getting my license. *Not every landlord or property owner has their license*. You might think how can this thought be helpful, and I'll explain.

It was helpful to me, because I knew that I was heading down a path that was unlike any other before. I knew at that exact moment that if the state of Nevada denied me because of my past, I could use the experience of real estate school to work with someone who's licensed and invest the money I earned to build generation wealth.

That is why I had a sense of peace about the journey, and I can promise you that thought was placed into my head by the Holy Spirit inside of me. If you were biting your nails in anxiety, you can stop, because I'm not sure if I would have written this book if I was denied my license. The very definition of faith is "believing without seeing," and that's what I expressed that day I prayed and then pursued real estate.

I shudder to imagine where I would be if I had let those five seconds of doubt and fear prevent me from at least trying to get my license. After I passed the final exams to get my license in October of 2019, I had to figure out which brokerage/company I wanted to partner up with. Before that though, the journey to Maui for Halloween 2019 shone as a beacon of hope, reminding us of the transformative power of redemption. It was not merely a vacation but a divine blessing bestowed upon us, a testament to the remarkable second chances life can offer. For within the depths of my past, a tumultuous chapter haunted by the shadows of addiction, lay the remnants of a life teetering on the precipice of tragedy.

As we stepped foot onto the shores of Maui, a sense of gratitude washed over us like the gentle caress of the ocean breeze. The vibrant colors of the island seemed to whisper tales of renewal and rebirth, reminding us that even in the darkest of times, there is a flicker of light that can guide us back to the path of righteousness.

The Lahaina yacht club, with its bustling energy and captivating festivities, became a sanctuary where our souls could revel in the joy of newfound freedom. Surrounded by loved ones, their unwavering support serving as an anchor in the stormy seas of recovery, we embarked on a journey of healing and self-discovery. The extravagant costumes and jubilant parades became a poignant reminder of the metamorphosis we had undergone, shedding the shackles of addiction to embrace a life of purpose and authenticity.

Every step along the vibrant strip was a testament to the grace that had been bestowed upon us. The laughter and camaraderie we shared with strangers became a tangible reminder of the interconnectedness of humanity, of the collective resilience that can arise from the depths of despair. It was as if God, in His infinite wisdom, had orchestrated this divine symphony of love and redemption, bringing together souls who had traversed their own treacherous paths and emerged stronger, wiser, and filled with compassion.

The dinner at the Lahaina yacht club took on a sacred quality, as the flavors on our plates mirrored the richness of our transformed lives. Each bite became an offering of gratitude, a testament to the healing power of forgiveness and the boundless mercy that had been bestowed upon us. We shared stories and laughter, basking in the warmth of newfound serenity and the profound understanding that we were indeed vessels of hope, walking testaments of the miracles that can unfold when we surrender ourselves to a higher power.

As the night drew to a close, we stood together, humbled by the journey that had led us to this moment. The haunting shadows of the past seemed but a distant memory, eclipsed by the radiant light of the present. In the embrace of Maui's vibrant Halloween celebration, we discovered that our past, though marked by darkness, was not a life sentence, but rather a catalyst for transformation. And in this realization, we found solace, knowing that our journey, once mired in tragedy, had been blessed by the divine touch of grace.

Thus, the time spent in Maui for Halloween 2019 transcended the realm of mere adventure. It became a sacred pilgrimage, a testament to the unwavering love and compassion of a higher power, and a resounding affirmation that even in the face of our darkest struggles, redemption is possible, and blessings can emerge from the ashes of our past.

After I got back, I decided to join Keller Williams, but I still had to send my application to the real estate division board down in Las Vegas. That fear of rejection that I escaped came rushing back, and I knew this was make or break. I didn't want to just be another application with a background check, so I wrote them a cover letter explaining my past, and then, I attached my Teen Challenge graduation certificate.

Once they approved my license application, I finally knew I wasn't crazy and that I was really living within God's will. That doesn't mean everything was happily ever after. I had my license for nine months before I received my first commission check, which was a whole new stress.

Yes, I was homeless at one point in my life, living every day from high to high, always having to steal for my money, but this time, I was free from all of that. There were a couple of times where I had the urge to go find some bartending job like I had in North Carolina, but each time, I was reminded God had placed me where I was supposed to be, so I just kept trying until I eventually closed my first transaction in August 2020. It was a $25,000 piece of land in one of the most rural parts I've ever been to.

They say the first one is always the hardest, and once you get it out of the way, the rest come easier, and I'd say, there is some truth to that statement. My very next transaction was with a very lovely couple from Ohio. This home was a special one, because the first time the couple saw it was the day after they bought it. I found them a wonderful home for $465,000, and in a blink of an eye, my life as a trusted realtor was cemented and my past life as a good for nothing junkie was completely erased. The day the escrow closed and I was able to hand over the keys to my buyers was one day I will hold near and dear to my heart forever and ever.

The couple broke out in tears and gave me the biggest hug. The feeling of love I felt coming from them was more intense than any shot of drugs I had ever injected. If there was ever a way to wipe away every terrible thing I did in my past, this had to be it.

You might find this surprising, but the money I made from helping them was about half of what I was used to making for brokering deals between growers and medical dispensaries.

The little devil on your shoulder may never go away and I want to remind you of a saying he's known for. "The grass is always greener on the other side." Why might that be? I personally believe it's because you/we are spending too much time thinking about "what ifs" and comparing our lives to others instead of simply realizing things take time and we have to worry about our grass and making it as green as we possibly can.

This cold November day was a major moment in my life as it reignited my love for helping people. As you read before, I moved to Charlotte specifically to become a missionary, so I've always had a love for helping people.

In that exact moment, I knew this was why God brought me from the east coast to the west coast, and I couldn't be more positive that I was now living in my calling. It hasn't stopped there either. I can hardly believe how far I've come. Since those first transactions that kick-started my career in real estate, I've gone on to sell millions and millions of dollars' worth of homes. While the specifics may have changed since the publication of my book, the biggest single transaction I've closed since letting go and letting God has been $750,000. And my biggest month? A staggering $825,000.

But that's only one part of the story. In the spring of 2022, my wife and I purchased our first rental property. It was a pivotal moment for me in my faith journey, as I had a vision but didn't know how to bring it to fruition. The pandemic provided me with ample reading time, and I taught myself everything I could about real estate investing. It hasn't been easy, but with each passing month, I feel more confident that I'm walking the path that God has set for me.

There are moments when divine intervention intertwines with our own journeys, and this was the case in the winter of 2021! Wild Coincidences create extraordinary connections that can only be attributed to a higher power. Such was the case when, in a remarkable turn of events, God blessed me with the presence of my cousin, a male relative with whom I hadn't lived in the same city since we were just children of seven years old.

Reno, a city nestled in the heart of Nevada, became the stage upon which this extraordinary reunion unfolded. The odds seemed astronomical, as my cousin resided in Vail, Colorado—a place quite distant from the familiar streets I now called home. Yet, through divine orchestration, his path intersected with mine in a manner that could only be described as serendipitous.

As I reflect upon this remarkable occurrence, I am struck by the profound significance it holds in my journey of recovery. It was as if God, in His boundless wisdom and compassion, had recognized the importance of familial connection and the power it holds to heal and strengthen us.

With the arrival of my cousin, a profound sense of comfort and familiarity washed over me. We shared childhood memories, creating a bridge that spanned the years of separation. In his presence, I felt a sense of belonging and acceptance that was instrumental in my ongoing journey in recovery.

Together, we embarked on a new chapter, supporting and encouraging one another as we navigated the challenges of life. His presence became a reminder of the strength of family ties, of the unbreakable bond that withstands the test of time and distance.

In this reunion, I witnessed the hand of divine providence, marveling at the way God orchestrates our lives with precision and purpose. The arrival of my cousin in Reno, from a place so far removed, was a testament to the blessings that can emerge when we surrender ourselves to a higher power.

Through our shared experiences and the newfound camaraderie that blossomed, my cousin became not just a relative, but a pillar of support, a beacon of hope during the moments of doubt and struggle. His presence served as a reminder that even in the midst of our darkest moments, God can bless us with unexpected connections that bring solace, strength, and renewed determination.

As I continue on my journey of recovery, I am grateful for the divine intervention that brought my cousin to Reno, a reminder that God's love and guidance extend far beyond our comprehension. Together, we face the challenges ahead, bolstered by the unbreakable bond of family and the knowledge that God works in mysterious ways, bringing blessings and support when we need them most.

Along the way, I've also been blessed with the support of my wife's family. My mother-in-law and mother have been instrumental in helping me prepare for the next chapters of my life. And I've even had the opportunity to partner with my mother-in-law, which has been a tremendous blessing.

When my wife and I got married, it was a long-awaited event that had been two years in the making. Although we didn't plan for it to take that long, the restrictions on gatherings due to COVID-19 made us want to wait until it was safe for everyone to celebrate together.

Unfortunately, we experienced unexpected losses along the way. Both of my grandparents on my mother's side passed away, and it was a heart-wrenching experience knowing that they wouldn't be there to see us exchange our vows. I had always prayed that God would bless me with a wife and that my grandparents would have the opportunity to meet her. Luckily, they were able to meet her, even if only during our engagement period. Their presence in our lives was a blessing in itself, and it meant the world to me.

My grandfather passed away shortly after our engagement, and we didn't have the chance to celebrate with them as his funeral took precedence. We moved our original wedding date from November 2021 to May 2022 and attended my grandmother's funeral instead. Although it may seem sad, we found comfort in knowing that they lived amazing lives filled with laughter and adventure.

After putting those difficult times behind us, we focused on the wedding planning. I asked my father, brother, uncle, cousin, and close friend to stand beside me at the altar. The next step was to find the perfect venue to hold all our guests, and my wife proved to be a true superstar in helping to make it happen.

My work was keeping me extremely busy, and I relied heavily on her to handle the crucial details. After looking at several venues, we decided on The Elm Estate, which had gated grounds that could hold a party of a little over 100 people. They even had charming cottages on the property where our traveling family members could stay over the weekend.

Sending out the invitations was another task that felt overwhelming, and it seemed like we were always missing a few people while trying to finalize the guest list. However, we managed to send them out and eagerly awaited the big day.

When the wedding day finally arrived, I was a bundle of nerves. In my anxiety, I left our marriage certificate at home, and we had to send our friend Franklin to retrieve it. It wasn't necessary, as it turned out, since our close friend G was the one who officiated the wedding and would have signed it the following day.

As I look back on that day, I am grateful for my wife, my family, and my friends who helped make it all happen. The challenges we faced along the way only made our wedding day more special, and I learned that even when we do our best, things will still go wrong. But as long as we keep our focus on what truly matters, we can weather any storm.

There are moments when divine blessings grace our lives, weaving a narrative that exceeds our wildest expectations. Such was the case when, a little over a year after our marriage, God bestowed upon my wife and me a precious gift—Minnie, a gorgeous miniature poodle mix who would forever alter the course of our journey.

From the very first moment we laid eyes on her, it was evident that Minnie possessed a captivating charm that surpassed her petite frame. Her velvety fur, adorned with the hues of caramel and cream, shimmered under the soft glow of sunlight. But it was her intelligence and gentle spirit that truly stole our hearts.

As we welcomed Minnie into our lives, we soon discovered that she was more than just a beloved companion. In her own remarkable way, she became an unexpected guide, leading us toward a new chapter of growth and responsibility. With each playful wag of her tail and every soulful gaze, Minnie helped prepare us for the future role of parenthood that awaited us.

Through Minnie's presence, we learned the invaluable lessons of patience, selflessness, and unconditional love. Her intuitive nature seemed to anticipate our needs, offering comfort during moments of stress or uncertainty. In her gentle eyes, we glimpsed the unwavering loyalty that would guide us through the joys and challenges of raising a child.

Minnie's intelligence astounded us. She quickly mastered commands, responding with a grace and attentiveness that belied her small stature. It was as if she understood the profound importance of her role in our lives, recognizing that she was not only a beloved pet but also a bridge between our aspirations and the dreams we held in our hearts.

As we embarked on the journey of dog parenthood, Minnie became a beacon of unwavering support and companionship. She is walking alongside us through the joys and tribulations, reminding us to cherish each moment and to embrace the transformative power of love.

Looking back, it's clear that my success is not solely the result of my hard work and determination. It's the product of surrendering to God and allowing Him to guide me in the direction He wants me to go. And while I may not know what the future holds, I am filled with a sense of peace and purpose, knowing that I am exactly where I am supposed to be.

Life seems uncontrollable when you are young, and I think that's why most of us grow up with what some people would call OCD. Personally, I found the most freedom in just accepting the fact that life is more peaceful when you don't care about the things that are out of your control.

When I realized no matter what I do I will never have the power to keep someone from speaking bad about me, I felt freedom. I can promise you that the only opinion you should ever worry about is God's. If you have anything going on in your life that you've tried changing or fixing over and over and you just keep failing, listen to this next piece of advice.

It's Okay to Struggle, but not in Silence

The struggle ends when we die! No matter how successful we become, struggles will always be present, albeit in different forms.

For me, life is about minimizing our mistakes in the present and maximizing good choices. It's about learning from our mistakes and striving to do better. It's about making the most of every opportunity that comes our way and using our experiences to become better versions of ourselves.

One of the most challenging aspects of my journey toward recovery was learning to let go of the toxic influences that had surrounded me in the past. As I embarked on the path toward sobriety, I realized that I could no longer maintain the relationships with those who had enabled and encouraged my addiction.

It was a difficult decision to make, and one that left me feeling isolated and alone. Yet, I knew that in order to truly embrace the transformation that lay before me, I needed to distance myself from those who represented the darker chapters of my past.

It was during this tumultuous period that I discovered the true power of faith. In the depths of my despair, I found solace in the knowledge that God was with me every step of the way, guiding me toward a brighter future.

And so, as I emerged from the cocoon of rehabilitation, I was blessed with a newfound sense of purpose and direction. I no longer felt the need to rely on the toxic influences that had defined my past, and instead, I embraced the opportunity to forge new connections and relationships.

It was at this time that I met Amanda and her amazing friends. Their kindness, compassion, and unwavering support provided the foundation for a new chapter in my life. They helped me rediscover the joys of living a sober life, and provided the encouragement I needed to stay on track.

As I reflect upon the journey that brought me to this moment, I am filled with a profound gratitude for the blessings that have been bestowed upon me. Through the power of faith, I was able to overcome the obstacles that had once seemed insurmountable. And in doing so, I was rewarded with a new family of friends who have become an integral part of my journey.

In the end, it was my willingness to let go of the toxic relationships of the past that allowed me to embrace the new opportunities that awaited me. Through the guidance of God, I was led toward a brighter future, and surrounded by individuals who have become instrumental in my ongoing journey toward recovery.

While we cannot always control the circumstances that life throws our way, we can control our response to them. We can choose to dwell on our mistakes and let them define us, or we can choose to learn from them and move forward with wisdom and humility.

Ultimately, life is a journey of growth and self-discovery. It's about becoming the best version of ourselves and using our experiences to make a positive impact in the world. And even though we may still make mistakes along the way, we can take comfort in the fact that we are constantly learning and growing.

Through it all, I have come to understand that God has a way of erasing our past and allowing us to leave it behind.

In the midst of our struggles and failures, it can be easy to get caught up in the past and dwell on our mistakes. But God's grace is greater than our past, and He has the power to redeem even the most broken of situations. He can take our pain and turn it into something beautiful, something that can be used for His glory.

As C.S. Lewis once said, "You can't go back and change the beginning, but you can start where you are and change the ending." This quote has become a guiding principle in my life. I cannot change the past, but I can choose to leave it behind and start fresh in the present.

You aren't meant to change it on your own, but only you can begin the change. It won't be easy, but nothing worth doing in life is ever easy. Also, nobody knows why bad things happen to good people, but we must do our very best to prevent it from ruining the rest of our lives. The only thing for certain is that when you surround yourself with good kind people who truly love and care for you, any past trauma can easily be overcome, and that place was Teen Challenge and their home church Cross Tabernacle.

However, some people have been harmed and abused by others in their church they grew up in and therefore struggle with Christianity, but I'm here to tell you a church is just a big congregation of people under one roof loving on each other and worshipping their Lord and Savior. Now, whether that's at a Catholic church or a Baptist church or your best friend's backyard where everyone gathers around isn't important.

A musician might say going to a music festival is a form of church, and I would have to agree with them. They go to meet up with other families who are stressed from their daily lives simply wanting to fill up their empty cups. In between music sets everyone discussing their struggles and how we can help each other. Comparing the two can be a very hard thought to wrap your head around seeing as there were drugs and alcohol at Woodstock. What I want you to look at is the bigger picture. People hurting on the inside looking for answers in any way they can. The same way I went through Teen Challenge to become healed.

For me, it's extremely easy to want to try and cover up the pain instead of dealing with it, which is why I was so attracted to the underground scene. In my eyes, stress is a form of pain, and if you don't believe me, just look at how many people have died from alcohol over the last 100 years. It seems like instead of taking ownership of the thing that's caused you to lean on drugs, we get more stressed about our addiction, and that leads us into darker depths than one never thought possible, like shooting up morphine at the age of 17.

Your thing might be childhood trauma like sexual abuse, bullying, or it could be from loneliness. Don't make the same mistakes that I did. Instead of facing the stress of my future head on and the realization that nobody in my family thought I was going into the MLB, which had been my childhood plan, I chose to escape through drugs. With that being said, I would never change my past, because it led me to the amazing rehab, which in turn sent me on a path that has brought me countless blessings.

Wandering around the great plains and mountains to get away from the distractions of what your childhood environment says you should be in order to find out who you want to be is the American Dream! What happens along the journey causes you to realize who you are and what you stand up for is the exciting part of life, and then the real work begins, because if we all aren't working in one accord toward one mission of making the world more loving, caring, compassionate, and to be more like Jesus Christ showed us to be, the change won't happen. For me, I got on the bus and started wandering the states when I was 16.

At that time in my life, everywhere I looked was a big question mark. Everyone around me had the same questions about my future that I had, and the not knowing drove me crazy. My mountains and plains were fairgrounds, farms, military bases, and every coast of the country. I'm proud to say I'm a Christian, and following God has extended my life beyond what I had ever envisioned. After all, I thought I was destined to join the forever 27 club and look at what just five years following Him outside of rehab has brought me in the form of blessings.

My wife, my parents, and other family back into my life and a future with the possibility to be a dad and full of twists and turns and excitement and love from everywhere I turn. All of these things were so far out of my grasp in my heroin fentanyl addiction, I would think about ending it all on a daily basis, and you might ask why I still enjoy concerts. Well, I say to that, if you fail to stand firm in your beliefs, you will go wherever the wind blows, and that might just be a house full of needles!

I am humbled and honored that people want to hear my story of how God has transformed me into a loving husband and a man who knows how to help others. My journey has been one of ups and downs, but through it all, God has been faithful in His love and His guidance.

Growing up, I never imagined myself as a husband or a father. I was consumed by my own dreams and ambitions. It wasn't until I encountered God that my life began to change. Through the love and grace of Jesus Christ, I found healing and redemption. I began to understand the value of loving and serving others, and my heart began to soften toward the idea of marriage and family. Even with this newfound perspective, I still had much to learn about what it means to be a loving husband. When I met my wife, I was struck by her kind and gentle spirit, and I knew that I wanted to be the kind of man who could love her well.

At first, I struggled to overcome my selfish tendencies. I would often prioritize my own needs and desires over hers, and I didn't know how to communicate in a healthy and loving way. But through prayer and intentional effort, I began to make progress.

God used my wife to help me grow in areas where I was weak. Her patience, grace, and wisdom were invaluable as I learned how to be a more loving and selfless husband. She challenged me to see beyond myself and to consider the needs and desires of others.

As I began to grow in my marriage, I also felt a stirring in my heart to help others. God had been so gracious to me in my own life, and I knew that I wanted to extend that same grace and love to others. I began to explore ways that I could serve those in need. I volunteered at local shelters and soup kitchens, and I became involved in mentoring programs for at-risk youth. As I gave of myself to others, I found that my own heart was filled with a sense of purpose and joy. God continues to work in my heart, drawing me closer to Him and refining me into the man He wants me to be. Through prayer and reading the Bible, I began to understand His heart for the world and His desire for His children to love one another.

As I grow in my faith, I have found that my childhood passions are being reignited. I had always loved to write, and I began to feel a sense of urgency to share my story with others. I wanted to encourage those who may be struggling in their own journeys and to offer hope and guidance for those who may be feeling lost. It was during this time that my wife encouraged me to pursue my dream of writing a book. She believed in me when I didn't believe in myself, and she helped me to see that I had something valuable to offer to the world.

Over the course of the last year, I poured my heart and soul into writing a book that would share my story of transformation and offer practical advice for those who may be struggling in their own journeys. It was a labor of love, and I felt a deep sense of fulfillment as I wrote.

Thank you for reading about my experiences of addiction and the journey that led me to surrender my life to Christ. If this book motivates just one person to seek help, this book will be a tremendous success and another testament to God's glory! As I come to a close on this book and this chapter of my life, I am reminded that the trauma we face in life can either make us stronger or it can break us. If we choose to rise above our circumstances, we can become stronger than we ever thought possible. Though the journey may be long and winding, it is one worth taking. For it is through the twists and turns of life that we become who we were meant to be.

Remember, this is just my beginning, and it's your beginning, too, and you simply need to look in a strange place to be shown His light!

Printed in the USA
CPSIA information can be obtained
at www.ICGtesting.com
LVHW101542060823
754252LV00002B/18

9 798885 963954